D1501266

Spring Sonata

Sonata de primavera

Spring Sonata

Sonata de primavera

Ramón del Valle-Inclán

A Dual-Language Book

Edited and Translated by
STANLEY APPELBAUM

DOVER PUBLICATIONS, INC.
Mineola, New York

Bibliographical Note

This Dover edition, first published in 2005, contains the unabridged Spanish text of the work first published in 1904 by A. Marzo, Madrid, together with a new English translation by Stanley Appelbaum, who also wrote the Introduction and the footnotes.

Library of Congress Cataloging-in-Publication Data

Valle-Inclán, Ramón del, 1866–1936.
  [Sonata de primavera. English & Spanish]
  Spring Sonata = Sonata de primavera / Ramón del Valle-Inclán ; edited and translated by Stanley Appelbaum.
      p. cm. — (A dual-language book)
  ISBN 0-486-44071-0 (pbk.)
  I. Title: Sonata de primavera. II. Appelbaum, Stanley. III. Title. IV. Series.

PQ6641.A47S7513 2005
863'.62—dc22

2004060912

Manufactured in the United States of America
Dover Publications, Inc., 31 East 2nd Street, Mineola, N.Y. 11501

INTRODUCTION

Valle-Inclán: Life and Works

Ramón Valle Peña was born into a middle-class family in 1866 in the town of Villanueva de Arosa (province Pontevedra, region Galicia) in northwesternmost Spain. His father was a seaman and an amateur author. Young Ramón was steeped in the distinctive language and lore of his native region. In 1885, after completing secondary schooling in Pontevedra, he entered the University of Santiago de Compostela to study law, but remained only three years. He had already begun creative writing, however; the earliest published story traced by bibliographers dates to 1888. After the death of his father in 1890 he moved for a time to Madrid, where he contributed articles and stories to newspapers, and probably did the hackwork he refers to in his dedication (included in this Dover volume) to *Sonata de primavera.*

In 1892 he made his first visit to Mexico (under a year), where he wrote extensively and gathered impressions he would use in later works. Back in Pontevedra in 1893, he devoured French literature, cultivated a Bohemian appearance, and wrote steadily. His first book, *Femeninas,* a collection of six stories, appeared in Pontevedra in 1895. Late in 1896, he made a more lasting move to Madrid, where he became an habitué of literary coffeehouses. Wearing his hair and beard long, and dressing dramatically, he put on a brave show while living on an allowance barely sufficient to keep body and soul together. Fundamentally good-hearted and even shy, he came across as a poseur, yarn-spinner, swaggerer, and brawler. He concocted his pseudonym "del Valle-Inclán" out of ancestral family names, but was unable (in 1915) to acquire letters patent of nobility for lack of proof. In 1899, the year of his first play, *Cenizas* (Ashes), a coffeehouse altercation that became physical caused the loss of his infected left arm.[1]

---

1. His assailant was the critic and novelist Manuel Bueno (1874–1936).

A poseur, yes, but his writing was very good indeed, and he became friends not only with writers of the so-called Generation of 1898,[2] but also with the high priest of *modernismo,* the Nicaraguan-born Rubén Darío (1867–1916).[3] While continuing to write fine short stories, some of which were to supply material for subsequent longer works,[4] between 1901 and 1905 Valle wrote and published his highly regarded *Sonatas* tetralogy, named after the four seasons, which are the subject of the second part of this Introduction. In 1904 he also published his delicate short novel *Flor de santidad* (Flower of Sainthood), with its pastoral Galician setting. When his first important play *El marqués de Bradomín: Coloquios románticos* (The Marquis of Bradomín: Romantic Conversations; based primarily on the *Autumn Sonata*) was performed in 1906 (it was published in 1907), the actress Josefina Blanco was in the cast; they fell in love and married in 1907 (they eventually had six children). The year 1907 was also the year of Valle's first slim volume of poetry, *Aromas de leyenda* (Fragrances of Legend), not the first, and far from the last, of his tributes to his beloved Galicia.

In 1908 and 1909 Valle published a trilogy of novels that take place during the second Carlist War in the 1870s.[5] Then, until the 1920s, he

---

2. Such as "Azorín" (José Martínez Ruiz, 1873–1967). Critics disagree as to whether Valle-Inclán belongs in this group. Certainly at this period of his career he didn't share their general mission to reevaluate the essence of Spanishness and restore their nation's greatness, at least morally. His pre–World War estheticism and frequent cynicism ran counter to the soul-searching, philosophical stance, and social consciousness characteristic of such thoroughgoing 98-ers as Azorín, Pío Baroja, and Unamuno. Nevertheless, Valle-Inclán was serious under the surface, and proved to be more lastingly in the avant-garde than the canonical 98-ers.   3. *Modernismo,* essentially a Spanish-American literary movement imported into Spain at some remove in time, was an art-for-art's sake, sometimes precious, amalgam of such earlier French trends as the Parnassian movement and Symbolism. Valle-Inclán was to become the outstanding Spanish-born *modernista,* and Darío himself wrote the sonnet of praise which precedes the *Sonata de primavera.* The two men also shared an interest in theosophy. 4. The story "Beatriz" (1903), first called "Satanás" (Satan) in its 1900 version, is included in the 2004 Dover dual-language volume *Short Stories by the Generation of 1898* (ISBN 0-486-43682-9, same translator/editor). It shares a number of themes and motifs with the *Sonata de primavera.*   5. Like American authors loyal to the lost cause of the Confederacy, Valle was obsessed with the Spanish Carlist Wars, sympathizing with the the the unsuccessful pretenders to the throne. When Fernando (Ferdinand) VII died in 1833, he left his throne to his infant daughter Isabel (Isabella II) after altering the laws of succession to permit a female monarch. His brother Carlos (Charles) began a civil war that lasted until 1839. Later, after the 1868 revolution in which Isabel was ousted, the grandson of the earlier pretender, another Carlos, reopened hostilities. The power base of the Carlists was in the north, and the pretenders' chief support came from the clergy and the rural landowning nobility.

was chiefly active as a playwright (his plays will be discussed in meaningful groups, beginning with the next paragraph). In 1910 he toured the southern half of South America with his wife and with another major troupe. During the First World War, he sympathized with the Allies, and was invited to France in 1916 as a correspondent; he recounted his experiences in the 1917 book *La media noche* (Midnight). Also in 1916, he published his major statement on esthetics, the book of essays *La lámpara maravillosa* (The Magic Lamp). His other two verse collections appeared in 1919—*La pipa de kif* (The Hashish Pipe), avant-garde poems of urban life—and 1920—*El pasajero* (The Wayfarer), occult poems.

Valle's plays, the most forward-looking in Spain in the first third of the twentieth century (along with those of Lorca, his junior by 32 years), range from high tragedy to irreverent farce and disconcerting oddities.[6] The three plays that comprise the *Comedias bárbaras* (Barbaric Comedies; 1922, 1907, and 1908, in trilogy sequence) concern the rebellious family of the Galician feudal landowner Juan Manuel Montenegro, who had already appeared in the *Autumn Sonata* as the uncle of the Marquis of Bradomín; the outstanding play in this group is *Romance de lobos* (Ballad of Wolves; 1908), a stirring family tragedy. Three separate *modernista* verse plays, one with commedia dell'arte characters, appeared between 1909 and 1913.

Three farces, two of them in verse, were combined in the 1926 collection *Tablado de marionetas* (Marionette Theater): *Farsa italiana de la enamorada del rey* (Italian Farce of the Girl in Love with the King; 1920), the prose *Farsa infantil de la cabeza del dragón* (Child's Farce of the Dragon's Head; 1909), and the wickedly satirical *Farsa y licencia de la reina castiza* (Licentious Farce of the Genuinely Spanish Queen; 1920), about the promiscuous Isabel II and her propensity to write hot love letters, leaving herself open to blackmail (Valle sent a copy to her grandson, Alfonso XIII).

The "puppet show" volume of 1927, *Retablo de la avaricia, la lujuria y la muerte* (Puppet Plays of Avarice, Lust, and Death), combines five varied items (including two shadow plays and two mari-

---

6. Valle's bibliography is so complex, largely because of his practice of writing belated "prequels" to pre-existing works, and of republishing works in new combinations, sometimes with altered titles, that in this Introduction, to prevent bibliographical overload, his plays (and not all of them, by any means; they number over 20) will be mentioned by their definitive titles (only) in their definitive published groupings (the way they are available today, when they are). The years in parentheses are those of the first appearance of a play, either produced, published in a periodical, or published in a volume.

onette melodramas), the most important of which is the tragedy *El embrujado* (The Bewitched Man; 1913).

Valle's most personal contribution to the theater, and the form most closely associated with his name, is the *esperpento* (nonsensical "fright"). In the four plays that he specifically labeled as *esperpentos* (though critics often extend the term to include other works from at least 1920 on, including the late novels), Valle maliciously distorts reality and language the way concave or convex funhouse mirrors distort images; the characters are often dehumanized victims of chance or fate. The first, and most highly regarded, of these four plays was the 1920 *Luces de bohemia* (Bohemian Luminaries), a weird picture of Valle himself and his coffeehouse cronies, in which he now exhibits a social awareness, sympathizing with striking workers, while also satirizing life in Spain as a distortion of European civilization. The other three specific *esperpento* plays, all concerning the military, which Valle despised, were combined in the 1930 volume *Martes de carnaval*, which can be translated either as "Shrove Tuesday" or as "Carnival Mars-es"; these prose plays are *Las galas del difunto* (The Dead Man's Finery; 1926), the exceptionally brilliant *Los cuernos de don Friolera* (Lieutenant "Trinket" Cuckolded; 1921), and the outrageous *La hija del capitán* (The Captain's Daughter; 1927).

In the farces, *esperpentos,* and his late oeuvre in general, Valle works magic with the Spanish language, using vocabulary from every imaginable source, including thieves' jargon, and terms from many geographical areas in which some form of Castilian is spoken. (He had always been a master of style.) Some of the plays deemed unstageable when first published have been produced successfully since the 1960s.

In 1921, Valle returned to Mexico for a few months, having been invited to participate in the centennial celebrations of the nation's independence. He brought back with him the material for what has been called his finest novel, and even the greatest of all his works, the 1926 *Tirano Banderas* (The Tyrant Banderas), a portrait of an amoral Spanish-American dictator that was to influence such major New World novelists as Miguel Ángel Asturias, Alejo Carpentier, and Gabriel García Márquez, to mention just a few.

In 1927 Valle began publishing what he planned as a nine-volume series of novels, to be called *El ruedo ibérico* (The Iberian Bullring), about the turbulent end of Isabel II's reign; only two novels were completed. Understandably, he also had run-ins with touchy General Miguel Primo de Rivera, dictator of Spain from 1923 to 1930. But,

though the general had seen fit to exile Unamuno to the Canary Islands, he tried not to take Valle too seriously, and when Valle was jailed for two weeks in 1929, it was for a very specific nonpolitical offense. By 1928 the writer had finally achieved a degree of financial security, and even comfort, but his health was poor.

The coming of the 1931 republic (Spain's second ill-fated attempt) made a lot of difference in Valle's life. In 1932, thanks to the new laws, he was able to divorce his wife (he kept the children). In the same year he acted briefly as Curator of National Artistic Treasures, and became president of Madrid's famous liberal club, the Ateneo. But the current publisher of his works went bankrupt, and he was forced to write for newspapers again. In 1933 he was named Director of the Spanish Academy of Fine Arts in Rome, but his illness prevented him from making a go of it. After a second try, he returned to Spain only to enter a hospital in Santiago de Compostela (1935). His last article was published in October of that year. In the first days of 1936 he died of cancer of the bladder, having refused last rites.

The *Sonatas*

The *Sonatas* have remained Valle's most popular works, with more written about them than about the rest of his oeuvre. They have always had detractors who found them "escape" writing, divorced from reality, artificial, mere literature feeding on other literature; or else, mere soft-core pornography. But quotations like the following from recent literary historians tell another story: "the pinnacle of Spanish modernist prose"; "the beginning of modern Spanish literature"; "one of the perfect gems of Spanish literature"; "a classic for those who can appreciate pure creation." The *Spring Sonata,* in particular, has been said to reveal "exceptional narrative gifts and extreme skill in its denouement."

The *Sonatas* were expanded, improved reworkings of various earlier stories and articles, motifs and obsessions: the family name Bradomín appears as early as 1889 in the story "A media noche" (At Midnight), and a "Virgin of Bradomín" is mentioned casually in the above-mentioned story "Beatriz." The first *Sonata* that Valle worked on was the *Sonata de otoño* (Autumn Sonata), begun in 1901 and published in 1902. The *Sonata de estío* (Summer Sonata) was published in 1903; the *Sonata de primavera* (Spring Sonata; the novel reprinted and newly translated here), in 1904, by A. Marzo, Madrid; and the

Sonata de invierno (Winter Sonata), in 1905. Separately or together, they bear the subtitle "Memorias del marqués de Bradomín" (Memoirs of the Marquis of Bradomín).

They are meant to be read in seasonal order, beginning with spring; each season reflects a stage in Bradomín's life, from youth to old age. Each *Sonata* is some critic's favorite, but the *Spring Sonata* is especially meritorious for its relentless, eventful narrative flow, which maintains great tension until the very end, unencumbered by excessive incident or authorial reflections, its descriptive passages solidly supporting the story line and characterizations. Unlike the other *Sonatas,* there is no riot of local color for its own sake, there is relatively little prurience or blasphemy, and there are hardly any exotic words in the vocabulary. Spanish bookstores in New York City currently sell three different editions of *Primavera* alone (aside from two editions of the *Sonatas* as a whole), whereas there are currently no separate editions of its three companions.

In emulation of Balzac, Valle in his oeuvre tried to create a miniature "human comedy," reintroducing certain characters into one work (of whatever genre) after another. It is said that almost 40 of the characters in the *Sonatas* reappear elsewhere. The Marquis of Bradomín, hero of the *Sonatas,* a *modernista* Don Juan,[7] a Nietzschean "superman," and a disciple of Huysmans's Des Esseintes in *À rebours* (Against the Grain), appears in about a dozen other works, some earlier, some later. Very dear to Valle's heart, the marquis was sometimes clearly the author's stand-in (as in *Luces de bohemia*), at other times (as in the *Sonatas*) a wish-fulfillment glorification of the nobility-obsessed Valle, and, at the same time, both an emblem of the good and bad in Spanish aristocracy and a tool for examining an author's relationship to the literature he is creating. The marquis's pride and feeling of intellectual and artistic superiority to those around him are also typical of *modernista* authors, inimical to bourgeois existence. Other characteristic *modernista* features in the novel are the predilection for illness, the morbid association of love and death, and the pervasive brooding landscapes. Tics peculiar to Valle, often recurring in his works, are the death of a child, the lecherousness of the clergy, and the folk sorcery reminiscent of Caribbean voodoo.

Particularly Valle's, and by no means typical of all *modernismo,* are

---

7. The traditional Spanish Don Juan figure was reassessed and resuscitated by more than one Generation of 1898 author; see Azorín's novelette *Don Juan* (1922), included in the Dover anthology cited in footnote 4.

his never-flagging humor and his lively dialogue, already indicative of the major playwright he would soon become.

When does the story (at the time of which Bradomín is in his early twenties) take place? The *Oxford Companion to Spanish Literature* unhesitatingly (and no doubt correctly) states "ca. 1830." The author's only indication is: "*en los felices tiempos del Papa-Rey.*" Now, in one annotated Spanish edition of "Beatriz," the term *Papa-Rey* (Pope-King) is glossed as Pius IX, who reigned from 1846 to 1878 ("because he was also ruler of the temporal Papal States"). This may possibly be true for that story, which definitely takes place well after the first Carlist War. But it is much too soon for this in the *Spring Sonata:* the *Summer Sonata,* in which Bradomín is a man in his prime, takes place after that war, but still most likely earlier than 1846. Apparently, *Papa-Rey* (at least in the *Spring Sonata*) does not refer to a specific pope (let alone Pius IX, who was conspicuously more liberal and less monarchical than his predecessors), but to any pope before the Risorgimento reduced papal holdings to Vatican City; and the translation in the main text of this volume reflects that conviction.

The town of Ligura, where the *Spring Sonata* takes place, is fictitious (Valle hadn't visited Italy, but had read about it, and had studied the Italian paintings in the Prado). Some commentators have said that, as described by Valle, it resembles Santiago de Compostela, where he had been a university student for three years.

This Dover edition includes not only the introductory sonnet by Rubén Darío (found in all editions), but also the very rare dedication (to the editor who "prepublished" many fragments of the *Autumn Sonata* in 1901 in the Madrid paper *Los Lunes del Imparcial*). One source indicates that this dedication appeared only in a 1905 Barcelona edition; another, that it appeared in editions between 1904 and 1922. Nowadays it is hard to find.

The present editor/translator has never encountered an annotated edition of the *Spring Sonata;* the Dover footnotes represent totally original research. Nor has he come across a copy of what is apparently the only previous English translation (together with the other *Sonatas*): *The Pleasant Memoirs of the Marquis of Bradomín: Four Sonatas,* translated by May Heywood Broun and Thomas Walsh, published by Harcourt, Brace, New York, in 1924.

Finally, for reference only, very concise summaries of the other *Sonatas* follow (in "seasonal" order, not in order of original publication):

Summer Sonata: Bradomín has been an émigré in London since fighting on the losing side in the first Carlist War. Trying to forget a romance that went wrong, he sails for Mexico, where a family estate is tied up in a lawsuit. Going ashore for a while in Yucatan, he meets la Niña Chole, a beautiful, wealthy Creole, and is attacked by a highway robber. When he rejoins his ship, Chole boards as well. In the harbor of Veracruz, her devoted African servant is killed during an exhibition fight against sharks, but she is unmoved. When Bradomín prepares to visit his estate, she asks to come along, disclosing that she is the wife of General Diego Bermúdez. They break their journey at a convent, where she allows herself to be taken for Bradomín's wife and they consummate their love while a bell tolls for a death. Now she fears her jealous husband will find out, but when Bradomín urges her to run away with him to his hacienda, she reveals her "unforgivable" secret: the general is also her father! During a funeral mass, a young bandit, betrayed by a companion, escapes justice by hiding in the sacristy. In his defense, Bradomín shoots two bounty hunters; Chole buys off the rest. Bradomín returns to his ship in Veracruz, after learning that his estate is near Grijalba, and can be reached more easily by sea. Chole, who is with him, beams on a handsome young man who is lucky at cards; she calms Bradomín's jealousy by informing him that the lad is a homosexual Russian prince (Bradomín regrets that he was never able to love boys or enjoy Wagner's music.) Near Grijalba the group meets festival crowds; a black man married to a former servant of Chole's offers them hospitality; and Chole, betting on a cockfight, loses three kisses to the Russian, but Bradomín gives him money instead. The general finds the errant couple, lashes Chole's face, and rides off with her. Reaching his estate, Bradomín finds it occupied by bandits; at night there is gunfire: a bandit has kidnapped Chole and has brought her there! She and Bradomín make love, as he reflects that the greatest joy results from being forgiving, and not pigheaded.

Autumn Sonata: In his native Galicia, Bradomín, in the autumn of his life, receives a letter from his pious cousin Concha, who, though only 31, is dying of tuberculosis; he has loved her since childhood, but hasn't seen her for two years; she had been married to an old man. He journeys to her eighteenth-century palace, and has a vision of a ghost (apparently) beckoning from a window. They sleep together, and Bradomín puts under her pillow some herbs given to him by a woman along the way. Concha, feeling better, announces a visit by their cousin Isabel and Concha's daughters, whom Isabel has been raising; Bradomín is to pretend that he has been lodging nearby with their

uncle, Juan Manuel Montenegro. Concha dreams that an archangel (divine forgiveness) leads her out of a labyrinth (carnal sin), but Bradomín is "not yet a believer." Old Juan Manuel falls from his horse and is dragged. Isabel and the girls arrive. Concha receives a severely reproachful letter from Bradomín's pious mother. Bradomín's attentions to Isabel make Concha jealous. During a tryst in his room, Concha dies; when Bradomín goes to Isabel's room for help, she thinks he has come to sleep with her—and he does. Later he carries Concha's body to her own bedroom. In the morning, Concha's daughters ask Bradomín to shoot the kite which has been menacing their doves; they take the dead kite to frighten their mother with it, and learn the terrible truth. Bradomín weeps to think that no other woman will ever love him so; he is like a god who has lost his worshippers.

Winter Sonata: Bradomín is now quite old and alone; almost all the women in his life are now dead. He is in Estella, the city in Navarre which was the headquarters and the "court" of the pretender "Carlos VII" during the second Carlist War, 1872–1876. To escape detection by his enemy, the priest of Santa Cruz, Bradomín adopts a disguise, visits the friar Ambrosio Alarcón, and meets an ambitious seminarist. The friar takes Bradomín to his lodgings, where the shrewish housekeeper is a sister to a woman once in the service of Bradomín's grandmother. The friar is the personal chaplain of "Queen" Margarita's lady-in-waiting María Antonieta Volfani, with whom Bradomín arranges a tryst while her husband is away. Volfani arrives, bringing Bourbon cavalry, and Carlos determines to renew hostilities. In Estella, a picador has supplanted Bradomín in the affections of another lady-in-waiting, the Duchess of Uclés. An adolescent daughter of Bradomín and the duchess is being raised in a convent. Volfani has a stroke. A granddaughter of Princess Gaetani (of the *Spring Sonata*), who has inherited that princess's hatred, warns Carlos against Bradomín. A fanatical priest threatens to kill two Russian tourists as heretics, and Carlos sends Bradomín on a mission to him to prevent this. On the way, Bradomín is shot in the left arm; in a convent, a nun he once knew tends to him, aided by a fifteen-year-old novice, who is attracted to him; the arm must be amputated [like Valle's own]. The nun carries out his mission, though the Russians weren't really in danger; one of them is the homosexual prince from the *Summer Sonata*. The nun berates Bradomín for allowing the novice to fall in love with him. There are strong clues that the girl is the above-mentioned daughter of Bradomín. The marquis realizes that the Carlist cause is

a lost one, but finds this poetically beautiful. The friar is wounded by the treacherous seminarist. María Antonieta selflessly nurses her husband, who has become childish, though she agrees to bid Bradomín farewell. The marquis is urged to write his memoirs (the four *Sonatas*). He tells María Antonieta that she will change her mind and stop sacrificing herself, but she remains firm, and he "says good-bye to his old self."

Spring Sonata

Sonata de primavera

Al señor marqués de Bradomín de Rubén Darío, su amigo

¡Marqués —como el divino lo eres—, te saludo!
Es el otoño y vengo de un Versalles doliente,
Hacía mucho frío y erraba vulgar gente,
El chorro de agua de Verlaine, estaba mudo.

Me quedé pensativo ante un mármol desnudo
Cuando vi una paloma que cruzó de repente,
Y por caso de cerebración inconsciente
Pensé en ti. Toda exégesis en este caso eludo . . .

Versalles melancólico, una paloma, un lindo
Mármol, un vulgo errante municipal y espeso,
Anteriores lecturas de tus sutiles prosas,

La reciente impresión de tus triunfos . . . Prescindo
De más detalles, para explicarte por eso
como autumnal te envío este ramo de rosas.

RUBÉN DARÍO

Dedicatoria

No hace todavía tres años vivía yo escribiendo novelas por entregas, que firmaba orgullosamente, no sé si por desdén, si por despecho. Me complacía dolorosamente la obscuridad de mi nombre y el olvido en que todos me tenían. Hubiera querido entonces que los libros estuviesen escritos en letra lombarda, como las antiguas ejecutorias, y que sólo algunos iniciados pudiesen leerlos. Esta quimera ha sido para mí como un talismán. Ella me ha guardado de las competencias

To the Marquis of Bradomín from His Friend Rubén Darío

Marquis—as the divine one you are—I salute you!
It is autumn and I am returning from an ailing Versailles;
it was very cold, and vulgar folk were roaming about;
Verlaine's jet of water was silent.

I stood musing before a nude marble
when I saw a dove suddenly fly by,
and in an instance of free association
I thought of you. I avoid any explanation in this instance . . .

Melancholy Versailles, a dove, a pretty
statue, a gross crowd of roaming townspeople,
earlier readings of your subtle prose,

the recent impression of your triumphs . . . I forgo
further details, in order to explain to you thereby
why I am sending you this autumnal bunch of roses.

RUBÉN DARÍO

Dedication

It is not yet three full years since I was earning my living by writing serialized novels, which I signed proudly, I don't know whether out of contempt or indignation. I took a sad pleasure in the obscurity of my name and the general oblivion I was cast into. At that time I would have liked my books to be written in Lombardic script,[1] like the old letters patent of nobility, so that only a few initiates could read them. That fancy has been like a talisman for me. It has protected me against

1. A handwriting style found in Italian manuscripts of the seventh through thirteenth centuries.

3

mezquinas, y por ella no he sentido las crueldades de una vida que fue toda de luchas. Solo, altivo y pobre, he llegado a la literatura sin enviar mis libros a esos que llaman críticos, y sin sentarme una sola vez en el corro donde a diario alientan sus vanidades las hembras y los eunucos del Arte. De alguien, sin embargo, he recibido protección tan generosa y noble, que sin ella nunca se hubieran escrito las *Memorias del Marqués de Bradomín*. Esa protección, única en mi vida, fue de un gran literato y de un gran corazón: He nombrado a don José Ortega Munilla.

Hoy quiero ofrecerle este libro con aquel ingenuo y amoroso respeto que cuando yo era niño ofrecían los pastores de los casales amigos, el más blanco de sus corderos en la casa de mi padre.

VALLE-INCLÁN

Nota

Estas páginas son un fragmento de las «Memorias Amables», que ya muy viejo empezó a escribir en la emigración el Marqués de Bradomín. Un Don Juan admirable. ¡El más admirable tal vez!

Era feo, católico y sentimental.

Anochecía cuando la silla de posta traspuso la Puerta Salaria y comenzamos a cruzar la campiña llena de misterio y de rumores lejanos. Era la campiña clásica de las vides y de los olivos, con sus acueductos ruinosos, y sus colinas que tienen la graciosa ondulación de los senos femeninos. La silla de posta caminaba por una vieja calzada: Las mulas del tiro sacudían pesadamente las colleras, y el golpe alegre y desigual de los cascabeles despertaba un eco en los floridos olivares. Antiguos sepulcros orillaban el camino y mustios cipreses dejaban caer sobre ellos su sombra venerable. La silla de posta seguía siempre la vieja calzada, y mis ojos fatigados de mirar en la noche, se cerraban con sueño. Al fin quedéme dormido, y no desperté hasta cerca del amanecer, cuando la luna, ya muy pálida, se desvanecía en el cielo. Poco después, todavía entumecido por la quietud y el frío de la noche,

petty rivalries, and thanks to it I haven't felt the cruelties of a life entirely compounded of struggles. Alone, haughty, and poor, I have come to literature without sending my books to those people known as critics, and without sitting down even once in the circle where the females and eunuchs of art daily nourish their vanity. Nevertheless, from one man I have received patronage so generous and noble that without it the *Memoirs of the Marquis of Bradomín* would never have been written. That patronage, unique in my life, was that of a great litterateur and a great heart: I refer to José Ortega Munilla.

Today I wish to offer him this book with the same candid and loving respect with which, when I was a boy, the shepherds from the farms of friendly neighbors used to offer the whitest lamb in their flock to my father in our home.

VALLE-INCLÁN

Note

These pages are a fragment of the *Pleasant Memoirs* which the Marquis of Bradomín began to write as an émigré when he was already very old. An admirable Don Juan. Perhaps the most admirable!

He was ugly, Catholic, and sentimental.

Night was falling when the post chaise passed beneath the Porta Salaria[2] and we began to cross the countryside, which was filled with mystery and distant sounds. It was the classic countryside of vines and olive trees, with its ruined aqueducts, and its hills that have the graceful swelling of women's breasts. The post chaise was traveling down an old highway. The mules in the team were shaking their collars heavily, and the merry, uneven tinkling of their harness bells was awakening an echo in the blossoming olive groves. Ancient tombs lined the road, and parched cypresses were casting their venerable shade upon them. The post chaise unflaggingly followed the old highway, and my eyes, weary of peering into the night, were closing in sleep. Finally I dozed off, not awakening until almost dawn, when the moon, already very pale, was vanishing in the sky. Shortly afterward, still numbed by the calm and

---

2. A city gate on the northern edge of Rome, where the Via Salaria (salt road) begins. This ancient road runs north and northeast until it reaches the Adriatic.

comencé a oír el canto de madrugueros gallos, y el murmullo bullente de un arroyo que parecía despertarse con el sol. A lo lejos, almenados muros se destacaban negros y sombríos sobre celajes de frío azul. Era la vieja, la noble, la piadosa ciudad de Ligura. Entramos por la Puerta Lorenciana. La silla de posta caminaba lentamente, y el cascabeleo de las mulas hallaba un eco burlón, casi sacrílego, en las calles desiertas donde crecía la yerba. Tres viejas, que parecían tres sombras, esperaban acurrucadas a la puerta de una iglesia todavía cerrada, pero otras campanas distantes ya tocaban a la misa de alba. La silla de posta seguía una calle de huertos, de caserones y de conventos, una calle antigua, enlosada y resonante. Bajo los aleros sombríos revoloteaban los gorriones, y en el fondo de la calle el farol de una hornacina agonizaba. El tardo paso de las mulas me dejó vislumbrar una Madona: Sostenía al Niño en el regazo, y el Niño, riente y desnudo, tendía los brazos para alcanzar un pez que los dedos virginales de la madre le mostraban en alto, como en un juego cándido y celeste. La silla de posta se detuvo. Estábamos a las puertas del Colegio Clementino.

Ocurría esto en los felices tiempos del Papa-Rey, y el Colegio Clementino conservaba todas sus premáticas, sus fueros y sus rentas. Todavía era retiro de ilustres varones, todavía se le llamaba noble archivo de las ciencias. El rectorado ejercíalo desde hacía muchos años un ilustre prelado: Monseñor Estefano Gaetani, obispo de Betulia, de la familia de los Príncipes Gaetani. Para aquel varón, lleno de evangélicas virtudes y de ciencia teológica, llevaba yo el capelo cardenalicio. Su Santidad había querido honrar mis juveniles años, eligiéndome entre sus guardias nobles, para tan alta misión. Yo soy Bibiena di Rienzo, por la línea de mi abuela paterna. Julia Aldegrina, hija del Príncipe Máximo de Bibiena que murió en 1770, envenenado por la famosa comedianta Simoneta la Corticelli, que tiene un largo capítulo en las Memorias del Caballero de Seingalt.

Dos bedeles con sotana y birreta paseábanse en el claustro. Eran viejos y ceremoniosos. Al verme entrar corrieron a mi encuentro:

cold of the night, I began to hear the crowing of early-rising cocks and the bubbling murmur of a brook which seemed to be awakening with the sun. In the distance, battlemented walls stood out black and somber against a sky of cold blue. It was the old, noble, pious city of Ligura.

We entered by the Porta Lorenziana. The post chaise was moving slowly, and the tinkle of the mules' bells awoke a mocking, almost sacrilegious echo in the deserted, grass-grown streets. Three old women, resembling three shades, were crouched expectantly at the still locked door of a church, but other faraway bells were already ringing for dawn mass. The post chaise followed a street of vegetable gardens, large buildings, and convents, an ancient street paved with resonant flagstones. Beneath the somber eaves the sparrows were fluttering, and at the far end of the street the lamp of a prayer niche was guttering. The slow pace of the mules allowed me to glimpse a Madonna. She held the Child on her lap, and the Child, laughing and nude, stretched out his arms to reach a fish that his mother's virginal fingers held up in the air to him, as if it were a naïve, heavenly game. The post chaise halted. We were at the gates of the Collegio Clementino.

This was taking place in those happy days when the pope was a temporal ruler,[3] and the Collegio Clementino still preserved all its special ordinances, privileges, and sources of income. It was still the retreat of illustrious men, it was still known as a noble archive of knowledge. For many years now, its rector had been an illustrious prelate: Monsignor Stefano Gaetani, bishop of Betulia, of the family of the Princes Gaetani. To that man, filled with evangelical virtues and theological science, I was bringing a cardinal's hat. His Holiness had seen fit to honor my youthful years by choosing me from among his noble guards[4] for such a lofty mission. I am a Bibiena di Rienzo in the line of my paternal grandmother: Giulia Aldegrina, daughter of Prince Massimo di Bibiena. The prince died in 1770, poisoned by the famous actress Simonetta Corticelli, who plays a large part in the memoirs of the Chevalier de Seingalt.[5]

Two beadles wearing cassocks and birettas were walking in the cloister. They were old and ceremonious. On seeing me enter, they ran up to meet me:

---

3. For a discussion of this expression and the time of the story, see the Introduction. 4. This corps of personal guards of the pope, every member of which was of the papal nobility, existed from 1801 to 1970.   5. *Marianna* Corticelli, a dancer (1747–ca. 1773), was a mistress of the notorious Giacomo (Jacopo) Girolamo Casanova de Seingalt (1725–1798).

—¡Una gran desgracia, Excelencia! ¡Una gran desgracia!

Me detuve, mirándoles alternativamente:

—¿Qué ocurre?

Los dos bedeles suspiraron. Uno de ellos comenzó:

—Nuestro sabio rector . . .

Y el otro, lloroso y doctoral, rectificó:

—¡Nuestro amantísimo padre, Excelencia . . . ! Nuestro amantísimo padre, nuestro maestro, nuestro guía, está en trance de muerte. Ayer sufrió un accidente hallándose en casa de su hermana . . .

Y aquí el otro bedel, que callaba enjugándose los ojos, ratificó a su vez:

—La Señora Princesa Gaetani, una dama española que estuvo casada con el hermano mayor de Su Ilustrísima: El Príncipe Filipo Gaetani. Aún no hace el año que falleció en una cacería. ¡Otra gran desgracia, Excelencia . . . !

Yo interrumpí un poco impaciente:

—¿Monseñor ha sido trasladado al Colegio?

—No lo ha consentido la Señora Princesa. Ya os digo que está en trance de muerte.

Inclinéme con solemne pesadumbre.

—¡Acatemos la voluntad de Dios!

Los dos bedeles se santiguaron devotamente. Allá en el fondo del claustro resonaba un campanilleo argentino, grave, litúrgico. Era el viático para Monseñor, y los bedeles se quitaron las birretas. Poco después, bajo los arcos, comenzaron a desfilar los colegiales: Humanistas y teólogos, doctores y bachilleres formaban larga procesión. Salían por un arco divididos en dos hileras, y rezaban con sordo rumor. Sus manos cruzadas sobre el pecho, oprimían las birretas, mientras las flotantes becas barrían las losas. Yo hinqué una rodilla en tierra y los miré pasar. Bachilleres y doctores también me miraban. Mi manto de guardia noble pregonaba quién era yo, y ellos lo comentaban en voz baja. Cuando pasaron todos, me levanté y seguí detrás. La campanilla del viático ya resonaba en el confín de la calle. De tiempo en tiempo algún viejo devoto salía de su casa con un farol encendido, y haciendo la señal de la cruz se incorporaba al cortejo. Nos detuvimos en una plaza solitaria, frente a un palacio que tenía todas las ventanas iluminadas. Lentamente el cortejo penetró en el ancho zaguán. Bajo la bóveda, el rumor de los rezos se hizo más grave, y el argentino son de la campanilla revoloteaba glorioso sobre las voces apagadas y contritas.

Subimos la señorial escalera. Hallábanse francas todas las puertas

"A great misfortune, Your Excellency! A great misfortune!"

I halted, looking at each one in turn:

"What's going on?"

The two beadles sighed. One of them began:

"Our learned rector . . ."

And the other, tearful but professorial, corrected him:

"Our most loving father, Excellency! . . . Our most loving father, our teacher, our guide, is on the verge of death. Yesterday, in his sister's house, he had a stroke . . ."

And here it was the turn of the other beadle, who had silently been drying his eyes, to amplify the statement:

"His sister the Princess Gaetani, a Spanish lady who was married to His Grace's elder brother, Prince Filippo Gaetani. It's not yet a year since he died on a hunt. Another great misfortune, Excellency! . . ."

I interrupted him somewhat impatiently:

"Has Monsignor been transferred to the Collegio?"

"The Princess wouldn't allow it. As I've told you, he's on the verge of death."

I bowed in solemn grief.

"Let us obey the will of God!"

The two beadles crossed themselves devoutly. There at the far end of the cloister a little bell was ringing, silvery, grave, liturgical. It was the viaticum for Monsignor, and the beadles doffed their birettas. Shortly afterward, underneath the arches, the members of the foundation began to parade by: humanists and theologians, doctors and bachelors, formed a long procession. They were coming out under an arch, divided into two files, praying with a muffled sound. Their hands, crossed on their chests, were clasping their birettas tightly, while their floating gowns swept the flagstones. I sank to one knee and watched them go by. The bachelors and doctors were looking at me, too. My noble guardsman's mantle proclaimed my identity, which they were commenting on in low tones. After they had all gone by, I arose and followed them. The viaticum handbell was already ringing at the far end of the street. Every so often some aged devotee would come out of his house with a lighted lantern and, making the sign of the cross, would join the cortege. We halted on a solitary square opposite a palace in which all the windows were lit. Slowly the cortege filed into the wide entranceway. Beneath its vaulting the sound of their prayers became deeper, and the silvery sound of the handbell hovered gloriously above the subdued, contrite voices.

We ascended the stately front stairs. All the doors were open, and ser-

y viejos criados con hachas de cera nos guiaron a través de los salones desiertos. La cámara donde agonizaba Monseñor Estefano Gaetani estaba sumida en religiosa oscuridad. El noble prelado yacía sobre un lecho antiguo con dosel de seda. Tenía cerrados los ojos: Su cabeza desaparecía en el hoyo de las almohadas, y su corvo perfil de patricio romano destacábase en la penumbra inmóvil, blanco, sepulcral, como el perfil de las estatuas yacentes. En el fondo de la estancia, donde había un altar, rezaban arrodilladas la Princesa y sus cinco hijas.

La Princesa Gaetani era una dama todavía hermosa, blanca y rubia: Tenía la boca muy roja, las manos como de nieve, dorados los ojos y dorado el cabello. Al verme clavó en mí una larga mirada y sonrió con amable tristeza. Yo me incliné y volví a contemplarla. Aquella Princesa Gaetani me recordaba el retrato de María de Médicis, pintado cuando sus bodas con el Rey de Francia, por Pedro Pablo Rubens.

Monseñor apenas pudo entreabrir los ojos y alzarse sobre las almohadas, cuando el sacerdote que llevaba el viático se acercó a su lecho: Recibida la comunión, su cabeza volvió a caer desfallecida, mientras sus labios balbuceaban una oración latina, fervorosos y torpes. El cortejo comenzó a retirarse en silencio: Yo también salí de la alcoba. Al cruzar la antecámara, acercóse a mí un familiar de Monseñor:

—¿Vos, sin duda, sois el enviado de Su Santidad . . . ?

—Así es: Soy el Marqués de Bradomín.

—La Princesa acaba de decírmelo . . .

—¿La Princesa me conoce?

—Ha conocido a vuestros padres.

—¿Cuándo podré ofrecerle mis respetos?

—La Princesa desea hablaros ahora mismo.

Nos apartamos para seguir la plática en el hueco de una ventana. Cuando desfilaron los últimos colegiales y quedó desierta la antecámara, miré instintivamente hacia la puerta de la alcoba, y vi a la Princesa que salía rodeada de sus hijas, enjugándose los ojos con un pañuelo de encajes. Me acerqué y le besé la mano. Ella murmuró débilmente:

—¡En qué triste ocasión vuelvo a verte, hijo mío!

La voz de la Princesa Gaetani despertaba en mi alma un mundo de recuerdos lejanos que tenían esa vaguedad risueña y feliz de los recuerdos infantiles. La Princesa continuó:

vants bearing wax torches led us across the deserted salons. The room in which Monsignor Stefano Gaetani lay in his death throes was plunged into religious darkness. The noble prelate was lying on an antique bed with a silk canopy. His eyes were closed. His head was sunk in the deep pit of the pillows, and his aquiline profile, that of a Roman patrician, stood out white and sepulchral in the motionless gloom like the profile of recumbent funerary statues. At the back of the room, where an altar was located, the princess and her five daughters were kneeling in prayer.

Princess Gaetani was a lady still beautiful, white-skinned and blonde. Her lips were very red, her hands as if made of snow, her eyes golden, her hair golden. On seeing me, she gazed at me for some time, smiling with an affable sadness. I bowed and continued to observe her. That Princess Gaetani reminded me of the portrait of Maria de' Medici painted on the occasion of her marriage to the king of France by Peter Paul Rubens.

Monsignor was barely able to open his eyes slightly and raise himself up on his pillows when the priest bearing the viaticum approached his bed. After he received communion, his head fell back again feebly, while his lips stammered a prayer in Latin, fervently but awkwardly. The cortege began to withdraw in silence. I, too, left the bedroom. As I was crossing the anteroom, one of Monsignor's familiars approached me:

"You are no doubt His Holiness's envoy . . . ?"

"True. I am the Marquis of Bradomín."

"The princess has just told me so . . ."

"The princess knows me?"

"She knew your parents."

"When can I pay her my respects?"

"The princess wishes to speak with you this very moment."

We drew aside to continue our conversation in a window recess. After the last members of the Collegio had marched past and the anteroom was empty, I instinctively glanced toward the bedroom door, and I saw the princess come out surrounded by her daughters, drying her eyes with a lace handkerchief. I went up to her and kissed her hand. She murmured faintly:

"On what a sad occasion I see you again, my son!"

Princess Gaetani's voice awakened in my soul a world of distant memories which partook of that pleasant, happy vagueness of childhood memories. The princess went on:

—¿Qué sabes de tu madre? De niño te parecías mucho a ella, ahora no . . . ¡Cuántas veces te tuve en mi regazo! ¿No te acuerdas de mí? Yo murmuré indeciso.

—Me acuerdo de la voz . . .

Y callé evocando el pasado. La Princesa Gaetani me contemplaba sonriendo, y de pronto, en el dorado misterio de sus ojos, yo adiviné quién era. A mi vez sonreí: Ella entonces me dijo:

—¿Ya te acuerdas?

—Sí . . .

—¿Quién soy?

Volví a besar su mano, y luego respondí:

—La hija del Marqués de Agar . . .

Sonrió tristemente recordando su juventud, y me presentó a sus hijas:

—María del Rosario, María del Carmen, María del Pilar, María de la Soledad, María de las Nieves . . . Las cinco son Marías.

Con una sola y profunda reverencia las saludé a todas. La mayor, María del Rosario, era una mujer de veinte años, y la más pequeña, María de las Nieves, una niña de cinco. Todas me parecieron bellas y gentiles. María del Rosario era pálida, con los ojos negros, llenos de luz ardiente y lánguida. Las otras, en todo semejantes a su madre, tenían dorados los ojos y el cabello. La Princesa tomó asiento en un ancho sofá de damasco carmesí, y empezó a hablarme en voz baja. Sus hijas se retiraron en silencio, despidiéndose de mí con una sonrisa, que era a la vez tímida y amable. María del Rosario salió la última. Creo que además de sus labios me sonrieron sus ojos, pero han pasado tantos años, que no puedo asegurarlo. Lo que recuerdo todavía es que viéndola alejarse, sentí que una nube de vaga tristeza me cubría el alma. La Princesa se quedó un momento con la mirada fija en la puerta por donde habían desaparecido sus hijas, y luego, con aquella suavidad de dama amable y devota, me dijo:

—¡Ya las conoces!

Yo me incliné:

—¡Son tan bellas como su madre!

—Son muy buenas y eso vale más.

Yo guardé silencio, porque siempre he creído que la bondad de las mujeres es todavía más efímera que su hermosura. Aquella pobre señora creía lo contrario, y continuó:

—María Rosario entrará en un convento dentro de pocos días. ¡Dios la haga llegar a ser otra Beata Francisca Gaetani!

"What news is there of your mother? When you were a boy, you looked a lot like her, but not now . . . How often I held you on my lap! Don't you remember me?"

I muttered vaguely.

"I remember your voice . . ."

And I fell silent, thinking of the past. Princess Gaetani was observing me with a smile, and suddenly, in the golden mystery of her eyes, I guessed who she was. It was my turn to smile. Then she said:

"Now you remember?"

"Yes . . ."

"Who am I?"

I kissed her hand again, then answered:

"The daughter of the Marquis of Agar . . ."

She smiled sadly, recalling her youth, and introduced me to her daughters:

"María del Rosario, María del Carmen, María del Pilar, María de la Soledad, María de las Nieves . . . All five are named María."

With a single deep bow I greeted them all. The eldest, María del Rosario, was a woman of twenty, and the youngest, María de las Nieves, a girl of five. They all looked beautiful and charming to me. María del Rosario was pale, with dark eyes that were full of an ardent but languid light. The others, who resembled their mother entirely, all had golden eyes and hair. The princess sat down on a wide sofa of crimson damask and began to speak to me in low tones. Her daughters withdrew in silence, taking leave of me with a smile that was shy and friendly at the same time. María del Rosario was the last to go out. I think that, besides her lips, her eyes smiled at me, too, but so many years have gone by that I can't state it as a certainty. What I do still remember is that, on seeing her move away, I felt a cloud of vague sadness covering my soul. For a moment the princess kept her eyes fixed on the door through which her daughters had departed; then, with that suavity of a lovable, pious lady, she said:

"Now you know them!"

I bowed:

"They're as lovely as their mother!"

"They're very good, which is more important."

I kept silent, because I've always believed that women's goodness is even more ephemeral than their good looks. That poor lady believed the opposite, and continued:

"María Rosario is to enter a convent in a few days. May God make her become a second Blessed Francesca Gaetani!"

Yo murmuré con solemnidad:

—¡Es una separación tan cruel como la muerte!

La Princesa me interrumpió vivamente:

—Sin duda que es un dolor muy grande, pero también es un consuelo saber que las tentaciones y los riesgos del mundo no existen para ese ser querido. Si todas mis hijas entrasen en un convento, yo las seguiría feliz . . . ¡Desgraciadamente no son todas como María Rosario!

Calló, suspirando con la mirada abstraída, y en el fondo dorado de sus ojos yo creí ver la llama de un fanatismo trágico y sombrío. En aquel momento, uno de los familiares que velaban a Monseñor Gaetani, asomóse a la puerta de la alcoba, y allí estuvo sin hacer ruido, dudoso de turbar nuestro silencio, hasta que la Princesa se dignó interrogarle, suspirando entre desdeñosa y afable:

—¿Qué ocurre, Don Antonino?

Don Antonino juntó las manos con falsa beatitud, y entornó los ojos:

—Ocurre, Excelencia, que Monseñor desea hablar al enviado de Su Santidad.

—¿Sabe que está aquí?

—Lo sabe, sí, Excelencia. Le ha visto cuando recibió la Santa Unción. Aun cuando pudiera parecer lo contrario, Monseñor no ha perdido el conocimiento un solo instante.

A todo esto yo me había puesto en pie. La Princesa me alargó su mano, que todavía en aquel trance supe besar con más galantería que respeto, y entré en la cámara donde agonizaba Monseñor.

El noble prelado fijó en mí los ojos vidriosos, moribundos, y quiso bendecirme, pero su mano cayó desfallecida a lo largo del cuerpo, al mismo tiempo que una lágrima le resbalaba lenta y angustiosa por la mejilla. En el silencio de la cámara, sólo el resuello de su respiración se escuchaba. Al cabo de un momento pudo decir con afanoso balbuceo:

—Señor Capitán, quiero que llevéis el testimonio de mi gratitud al Santo Padre . . .

Calló y estuvo largo espacio con los ojos cerrados. Sus labios, secos y azulencos, parecían agitados por el temblor de un rezo. Al abrir de nuevo los ojos, continuó:

—Mis horas están contadas. Los honores, las grandezas, las jerarquías, todo cuanto ambicioné durante mi vida, en este momento se esparce como vana ceniza ante mis ojos de moribundo. Dios Nuestro

I murmured solemnly:

"It's a separation as cruel as death!"

The princess interrupted me spiritedly:

"No doubt it's a very great sorrow, but it's also a comfort to know that the temptations and risks of the world no longer exist for one you hold dear. If all my daughters entered a convent, I'd be glad to follow them . . . Unfortunately, they're not all like María Rosario!"

She fell silent, sighing, her gaze distracted, and in the golden depths of her eyes I thought I saw the flame of a tragic, somber fanaticism. At that moment, one of the familiars who were keeping vigil by Monsignor Gaetani appeared at the bedroom door and remained there noiselessly, chary of disturbing our silence, until the princess deigned to question him, with a sigh in which contempt and affability were mingled:

"What's going on, Don Antonino?"

Don Antonino clasped his hands in false beatitude and turned up his eyes:

"What's going on, Excellency, is that Monsignor wishes to speak with His Holiness's envoy."

"Does he know he's here?"

"Yes, he does, Excellency. He saw him while he was receiving extreme unction. Even though one might think the opposite, Monsignor hasn't lost consciousness for a single minute."

Hearing all this, I had stood up. The princess held out her hand to me, and even at that crisis I managed to kiss it with more gallantry than respect. Then I entered the room in which Monsignor lay dying.

The noble prelate stared at me with his glassy, dying eyes and tried to bless me, but his hand fell back weakly alongside his body, while a tear trickled slowly and agonizingly down his cheek. In the silence of the room all that could be heard was his noisy breathing. After a moment he was able to say, in a painful stammer:

"Captain, I want you to take the assurance of my gratitude to the Holy Father . . ."

He fell silent and kept his eyes closed for some time. His dry, bluish lips seemed agitated by the tremor of a prayer. When he opened his eyes again, he went on:

"My hours are numbered. The honors, grandeur, rank, all that I strove for while I lived, are dispersed at this moment like vain ashes before my dying eyes. God our Lord has not abandoned me; he is

Señor no me abandona, y me muestra la aspereza y desnudez de todas las cosas . . . Me cercan las sombras de la Eternidad, pero mi alma se ilumina interiormente con las claridades divinas de la Gracia . . .

Otra vez tuvo que interrumpirse, y falto de fuerzas cerró los ojos. Uno de los familiares acercóse y le enjugó la frente sudorosa con un pañuelo de fina batista. Después dirigiéndose a mí murmuró en voz baja:

—Señor Capitán, procurad que no hable.

Yo asentí con un gesto. Monseñor abrió los ojos, y nos miró a los dos. Un murmullo apagado salió de sus labios: Me incliné para oírle, pero no pude entender lo que decía. El familiar me apartó suavemente, y doblándose a su vez sobre el pecho del moribundo, pronunció con amable imperio:

—¡Ahora es preciso que descanse Su Excelencia! No habléis . . .

El prelado hizo un gesto doloroso. El familiar volvió a pasarle el pañuelo por la frente, y al mismo tiempo sus ojos sagaces de clérigo italiano me indicaban que no debía continuar allí. Como ello era también mi deseo, le hice una cortesía y me alejé. El familiar ocupó un sillón que había cercano a la cabecera, y recogiendo suavemente los hábitos se dispuso a meditar, o acaso a dormir, pero en aquel momento advirtió Monseñor que yo me retiraba, y alzándose con supremo esfuerzo, me llamó:

—¡No te vayas, hijo mío! Quiero que lleves mi confesión al Santo Padre.

Esperó a que nuevamente me acercase, y con los ojos fijos en el cándido altar que había en un extremo de la cámara, comenzó:

—¡Dios mío, que me sirva de penitencia el dolor de mi culpa y la vergüenza que me causa confesarla!

Los ojos del prelado estaban llenos de lágrimas. Era afanosa y ronca su voz. Los familiares se congregaban en torno del lecho. Sus frentes inclinábanse al suelo: Todos aparentaban una gran pesadumbre, y parecían de antemano edificados por aquella confesión que intentaba hacer ante ellos el moribundo obispo de Betulia. Yo me arrodillé. El prelado rezaba en silencio, con los ojos puestos en el crucifijo que había en el altar. Por sus mejillas descarnadas las lágrimas corrían hilo a hilo. Al cabo de un momento comenzó:

—Nació mi culpa cuando recibí las primeras cartas donde mi amigo, Monseñor Ferrati, me anunciaba el designio que de otorgarme el capelo tenía Su Santidad. ¡Cuán flaca es nuestra humana naturaleza, y cuán frágil el barro de que somos hechos! Creí que mi estirpe de Príncipe valía más que la ciencia y que la virtud de otros varones:

showing me the coarseness and nakedness of all things . . . I am ringed about by the shadows of eternity, but my soul is illumined within by the divine brightness of Grace . . ."

Again he had to break off, and shut his eyes for lack of strength. One of his familiars approached and wiped his sweaty forehead with a fine cambric handkerchief. Then, addressing me, he murmured in low tones:

"Captain, try not to make him speak."

I assented with a gesture. Monsignor opened his eyes and looked at the two of us. A subdued murmur issued from his lips. I bent over to hear him, but I was unable to understand what he was saying. His familiar drew me away gently, and in his turn stooping over the dying man's breast, declared with friendly forcefulness:

"Now Your Grace must rest! Don't speak . . ."

The prelate made a sorrowful gesture. His familiar once again ran the handkerchief over his forehead, while his wise eyes, those of an Italian priest, indicated to me that I shouldn't remain there. Since it was also my own desire to leave, I bowed to him and moved away. The familiar sat down on an armchair that stood near the bedside and, gently gathering up his habits, prepared himself for meditation, or perhaps for a nap, but at that moment Monsignor noticed I was withdrawing and, raising himself with a supreme effort, he called:

"Don't go, my son! I want you to take my confession to the Holy Father."

He waited for me to approach again; then, staring at the white altar that stood at one end of the room, he began:

"My God, let it be as a penance to me, this grief over my fault, and the shame it costs me to confess it!"

The prelate's eyes were filled with tears. His voice was anxious and hoarse. His familiars assembled around the bed. Their foreheads were bent toward the floor. They all manifested great sorrow and seemed to be edified in advance by the confession which the dying bishop of Betulia was trying to make in their presence. I knelt. The prelate was saying a silent prayer, his eyes glued to the crucifix that stood on the altar. Down his emaciated cheeks the tears kept trickling. After a moment he began:

"My fault originated when I received the first letters in which my friend Monsignor Ferrati announced to me His Holiness's intention of bestowing the hat on me. How weak our human nature is, and how fragile the clay of which we are made! I thought that my princely lineage was more significant than other men's knowledge and virtue. Pride

Nació en mi alma el orgullo, el más fatal de los consejeros humanos, y pensé que algún día seríame dado regir a la Cristiandad. Pontífices y Santos hubo en mi casa, y juzgué que podía ser como ellos. ¡De esta suerte nos ciega Satanás! Sentíame viejo y esperé que la muerte allanase mi camino. Dios nuestro Señor no quiso que llegase a vestir la sagrada púrpura, y, sin embargo, cuando llegaron inciertas y alarmantes noticias, yo temí que hiciese naufragar mis esperanzas la muerte que todos temían de Su Santidad . . . ¡Dios mío, he profanado tu altar rogándote que reservases aquella vida preciosa porque, segada en más lejanos días, pudiera serme propicia su muerte! ¡Dios mío, cegado por el Demonio, hasta hoy no he tenido conciencia de mi culpa! ¡Señor, tú que lees en el fondo de las almas, tú que conoces mi pecado y mi arrepentimiento, devuélveme tu Gracia!

Calló, y un largo estremecimiento de agonía recorrió su cuerpo. Había hablado con apagada voz, impregnada de apacible y sereno desconsuelo. La huella de sus ojeras se difundió por la mejilla, y sus ojos cada vez más hundidos en las cuencas, se nublaron con una sombra de muerte. Luego quedó estirado, rígido, indiferente, la cabeza torcida, entreabierta la boca por la respiración, el pecho agitado. Todos permanecimos de rodillas, irresolutos, sin osar llamarle ni movernos por no turbar aquel reposo que nos causaba horror. Allá abajo exhalaba su perpetuo sollozo la fuente que había en medio de la plaza, y se oían las voces de unas niñas que jugaban a la rueda: Cantaban una antigua letra de cadencia lánguida y nostálgica. Un rayo de sol abrileño y matinal, brillaba en los vasos sagrados del altar, y los familiares rezaban en voz baja, edificados por aquellos devotos escrúpulos que torturaban el alma cándida del prelado . . . Yo, pecador de mí, empezaba a dormirme, que había corrido toda la noche en silla de posta, y cansa cuando es larga una jornada.

Al salir de la cámara donde agonizaba Monseñor Gaetani, halléme con un viejo y ceremonioso mayordomo que me esperaba en la puerta.

—Excelencia, mi Señora la Princesa me envía para que os muestre vuestras habitaciones.

Yo apenas pude reprimir un estremecimiento. En aquel instante, no sé decir qué vago aroma primaveral traía a mi alma el recuerdo de las cinco hijas de la Princesa. Mucho me alegraba la idea de vivir en el Palacio Gaetani, y, sin embargo, tuve valor para negarme:

arose in my soul, that most deadly of human counselors, and I imagined that some day I might rule over all Christians. There had been pontiffs and saints in my family, and I deemed I could be like them. This is how Satan blinds us! I felt myself growing old and I hoped that death would smooth my path. It was not the will of God our Lord that I should come to wear the sacred purple, but nevertheless, when uncertain, alarming news arrived, I feared lest my hopes be dashed by the death of His Holiness, which everyone feared . . . My God, I have profaned your altar by begging you to preserve that precious life in order that, when it was cut short in future days, his death could be of advantage to me! My God! Blinded by the devil, until this day I was unaware of my fault! Lord, you who read the depths of man's soul, you who know my sin and my repentance, restore your Grace to me!"

He fell silent, and a long shudder of agony shook his whole body. He had spoken in a faint voice imbued with peaceful, serene grief. The discoloration of the rings around his eyes spread to his cheeks, and his eyes, sinking deeper and deeper into their sockets, clouded over with a deathly shadow. Then he remained stiff, rigid, indifferent, his head twisted, his lips slightly parted by his respiration, his breast heaving. We all remained on our knees, irresolute, afraid to call to him or even to move, lest we disturb that repose which filled us with horror. Downstairs in the distance the fountain that stood in the middle of the square was emitting its perpetual sob, and we could hear the voices of some little girls playing a round game. They were singing an ancient text with a languid, nostalgic cadence. An April morning sunbeam was brightly reflected in the sacred vessels on the altar, and the familiars were praying in low tones, edified by those devout scruples which were tormenting the ingenuous soul of the prelate . . . I, sinner that I am, was beginning to doze off, for I had journeyed by post chaise all night long, and a long journey is tiring.

On leaving the room in which Monsignor Gaetani was dying, I found before me an old, ceremonious butler who was awaiting me by the door.

"Excellency, my lady the princess has sent me to show you to your quarters."

I could scarcely suppress a shudder. At that moment, some indefinable, vague scent of springtime wafted to my soul the recollection of the princess's five daughters. The idea of living in the Gaetani palace cheered me greatly, and yet I was courageous enough to refuse:

—Decid a vuestra Señora la Princesa Gaetani toda mi gratitud, y que me hospedo en el Colegio Clementino.

El mayordomo pareció consternado:

—Excelencia, creedme que le causáis una gran contrariedad. En fin, si os negáis, tengo orden de llevarle recado. Os dignaréis esperar algunos momentos. Está terminando de oír misa.

Yo hice un gesto de resignación:

—No le digáis nada. Dios me perdonará si prefiero este palacio, con sus cinco doncellas encantadas, a los graves teólogos del Colegio Clementino.

El mayordomo me miró con asombro, como si dudase de mi juicio. Después mostró deseos de hablarme, pero tras algunas vacilaciones, terminó indicándome el camino, acompañando la acción tan sólo con una sonrisa. Yo le seguí. Era un viejo rasurado, vestido con largo levitón eclesiástico que casi le rozaba los zapatos ornados con hebillas de plata. Se llamaba Polonio, andaba en la punta de los pies, sin hacer ruido, y a cada momento se volvía para hablarme en voz baja y llena de misterio:

—Pocas esperanzas hay de que Monseñor reserve la vida . . .

Y después de algunos pasos:

—Yo tengo ofrecida una novena a la Santa Madona.

Y un poco más allá, mientras levantaba una cortina:

—No estaba obligado a menos. Monseñor me había prometido llevarme a Roma.

Y volvió a continuar la marcha:

—¡No lo quiso Dios . . . ! ¡No lo quiso Dios . . . !

De esta suerte atravesamos la antecámara, y un salón casi oscuro y una biblioteca desierta. Allí el mayordomo se detuvo palpándose las faltriqueras de su calzón, ante una puerta cerrada:

—¡Válgame Dios . . . ! He perdido mis llaves . . .

Todavía continuó registrándose: Al cabo dio con ellas, abrió y apartóse dejándome paso:

—La Señora Princesa desea que dispongáis del salón, de la biblioteca y de esta cámara.

Yo entré. Aquella estancia me pareció en todo semejante a la cámara en que agonizaba Monseñor Gaetani. También era honda y silenciosa, con antiguos cortinajes de damasco carmesí. Arrojé sobre un sillón mi manto de guardia noble, y me volví mirando los cuadros que colgaban de los muros. Eran antiguos lienzos de la escuela florentina, que representaban escenas bíblicas —Moisés salvado de las aguas, Susana y los ancianos, Judith con la cabeza de Holofernes—. Para que

"Tell your lady, Princess Gaetani, how grateful I am, but I'll lodge at the Collegio Clementino."

The butler seemed dismayed:

"Excellency, trust me: you'd be vexing her enormously. But if you insist on declining, I have orders to bring you a message. Please be so good as to wait here a few moments. The mass she's attending is nearly over."

I made a gesture of resignation:

"Don't tell her a thing. God will forgive me if I prefer this palace, with its five enchanted maidens, to the grave theologians of the Collegio Clementino."

The butler looked at me in amazement, as if doubting I was in my right mind. Then he showed signs of wishing to address me, but after hesitating a few times, he finally led the way, accompanying the action with a mere smile. I followed him. He was old and clean-shaven, and wore a long ecclesiastical frock coat that nearly brushed his shoes, which were fitted with silver buckles. His name was Polonio; he walked on tiptoe, noiselessly, and turned around every minute to address me in a low, mystery-laden voice:

"There's very little hope of Monsignor's pulling through . . ."

And a few steps later:

"I have offered a novena to the Blessed Virgin."

And a little later, as he raised a curtain:

"That was the least I could do. Monsignor had promised to take me along to Rome."

And he set out again:

"It wasn't God's will! . . . It wasn't God's will! . . ."

In that manner we crossed the anteroom, a salon that was nearly pitch dark, and a deserted library. There the butler halted in front of a locked door, searching his trousers pockets:

"God help me! . . . I've lost my keys . . ."

Still he kept searching himself. Finally he found them, unlocked the door, and stood aside to let me enter:

"The princess desires that you avail yourself of the salon, the library, and this room."

I went in. That room appeared to me similar in every way to the one in which Monsignor Gaetani was dying. It, too, was deep and silent, with antique drapery of crimson damask. I tossed my noble-guards mantle onto an armchair, and turned around to look at the paintings hanging on the walls. They were antique canvases of the Florentine school depicting Bible scenes: Moses rescued from the river, Susanna and the elders, Judith with the head of Holofernes. So I could see them better, the butler ran from

pudiese verlos mejor, el mayordomo corrió de un lado al otro levantando todos los cortinajes de las ventanas. Después me dejó contemplarlos en silencio: Andaba detrás de mí como una sombra, sin dejar caer de los labios la sonrisa, una vaga sonrisa doctoral. Cuando juzgó que los había mirado a todo sabor y talante, acercóse en la punta de los pies y dejó oír su voz cascada, más amable y misteriosa que nunca:

—¿Qué os parece? Son todos de la misma mano . . . ¡Y qué mano . . . !

Yo le interrumpí:

—¿Sin duda, Andrea del Sarto?

El Señor Polonio adquirió un continente grave, casi solemne:

—Atribuidos a Rafael.

Me volví a dirigirles una nueva ojeada, y el Señor Polonio continuó:

—Reparad que tan sólo digo atribuidos. En mi humilde parecer valen más que si fuesen de Rafael . . . ¡Yo los creo del Divino!

—¿Quién es el Divino?

El mayordomo abrió los brazos definitivamente consternado:

—¿Y vos me lo preguntáis, Excelencia? ¡Quién puede ser sino Leonardo de Vinci . . . !

Y guardó silencio, contemplándome con verdadera lástima. Yo apenas disimulé una sonrisa burlona: El Señor Polonio aparentó no verla, y, sagaz como un cardenal romano, comenzó a adularme:

—Hasta hoy no había dudado . . . Ahora os confieso que dudo. Excelencia, acaso tengáis razón. Andrea del Sarto pintó mucho en el taller de Leonardo, y sus cuadros de esa época se parecen tanto, que más de una vez han sido confundidos . . . En el mismo Vaticano hay un ejemplo: La Madona de la Rosa. Unos la juzgan del Vinci y otros del Sarto. Yo la creo del marido de Doña Lucrecia del Fede, pero tocada por el Divino. Ya sabéis que era cosa frecuente entre maestros y discípulos.

Yo le escuchaba con un gesto de fatiga. El Señor Polonio, al terminar su oración, me hizo una profunda reverencia, y corrió con los brazos en alto, de una en otra ventana, soltando los cortinajes. La cámara quedó en una media luz propicia para el sueño. El Señor Polonio se despidió en voz baja, como si estuviese en una capilla, y salió sin ruido, cerrando tras sí la puerta . . . Era tanta mi fatiga, que dormí hasta la caída de la tarde. Me desperté soñando con María Rosario.

La biblioteca tenía tres puertas que daban sobre una terraza de mármol. En el jardín las fuentes repetían el comentario voluptuoso

side to side raising all the window curtains. Then he let me study them in silence. He walked behind me like a shadow, his smile never leaving his lips, a vague, professorial smile. When he deemed that I had looked at them to my heart's content, he drew near on tiptoe and let his cracked voice be heard, a voice more affable and mysterious than before:

"What do you think? They're all by the same hand . . . And what a hand! . . ."

I interrupted him:

"No doubt Andrea Del Sarto?"

Master Polonio assumed a grave, almost solemn countenance:

"Attributed to Raphael."

I cast another glance at them, and Master Polonio continued:

"Take note that I merely say 'attributed.' In my humble opinion they're more valuable than if they were by Raphael . . . I think they're by the divine one!"

"Who is the divine one?"

The butler spread out his arms, now altogether dismayed:

"And you ask me that, Excellency? Who could it be but Leonardo da Vinci?! . . ."

And he kept silent, observing me in genuine pity. I scarcely suppressed a mocking smile. Master Polonio pretended not to see it and, crafty as a Roman cardinal, he began to flatter me:

"Until today I never doubted . . . Now I confess to you that I have doubts. Excellency, you may be right. Andrea Del Sarto did a lot of painting in Leonardo's studio, and their pictures of that period are so much alike that they've been misidentified more than once . . . There's an example in the Vatican itself: the Madonna of the Rose. Some consider it to be by Da Vinci; others, by Del Sarto. I believe it to be by the husband of Donna Lucrezia del Fede, but retouched by the divine one. Of course you know that that was a frequent occurrence between masters and pupils."

I was listening to him with an expression of fatigue. When Master Polonio finished his speech, he made me a low bow and ran with upraised arms from one window to another, letting the curtains down. The room was left in a half-light that invited slumber. Master Polonio took his leave in low tones, as if he were in a chapel, and went out noiselessly, shutting the door behind him . . . I was so weary that I slept until evening was falling. When I awoke, it was from a dream of María Rosario.

The library had three doors which opened onto a marble terrace. In the garden the fountains were repeating the voluptuous commentary

que parecen hacer a todo pensamiento de amor, sus voces eternas y juveniles. Al inclinarme sobre la balaustrada, yo sentí que el hálito de la Primavera me subía al rostro. Aquel viejo jardín de mirtos y de laureles mostrábase bajo el sol poniente lleno de gracia gentílica. En el fondo, caminando por los tortuosos senderos de un laberinto, las cinco hermanas se aparecían con las faldas llenas de rosas, como en una fábula antigua. A lo lejos, surcado por numerosas velas latinas que parecían de ámbar, extendíase el Mar Tirreno. Sobre la playa de dorada arena morían mansas las olas, y el son de los caracoles con que anunciaban los pescadores su arribada a la playa, y el ronco canto del mar, parecían acordarse con la fragancia de aquel jardín antiguo donde las cinco hermanas se contaban sus sueños juveniles, a la sombra de los rosáceos laureles.

Se habían sentado en un gran banco de piedra a componer sus ramos. Sobre el hombro de María Rosario estaba posada una paloma, y en aquel cándido suceso yo hallé la gracia y el misterio de una alegoría. Tocaban a fiesta unas campanas de aldea, y la iglesia se perfilaba a lo lejos en lo alto de una colina verde, rodeada de cipreses. Salía la procesión, que anduvo alrededor de la iglesia, y distinguíanse las imágenes en sus andas, con los mantos bordados que brillaban al sol, y los rojos pendones parroquiales que iban delante, flameando victoriosos como triunfos litúrgicos. Las cinco hermanas se arrodillaron sobre la yerba, y juntaron las manos llenas de rosas.

Los mirlos cantaban en las ramas, y sus cantos se respondían encadenándose en un ritmo remoto como las olas del mar. Las cinco hermanas habían vuelto a sentarse: Tejían sus ramos en silencio, y entre la púrpura de las rosas revoloteaban como albas palomas sus manos, y los rayos del sol que pasaban a través del follaje, temblaban en ellas como místicos haces encendidos. Los tritones y las sirenas de las fuentes borboteaban su risa quimérica, y las aguas de plata corrían con juvenil murmullo por las barbas limosas de los viejos monstruos marinos que se inclinaban para besar a las sirenas, presas en sus brazos. Las cinco hermanas se levantaron para volver al Palacio. Caminaban lentamente por los senderos del laberinto, como princesas encantadas que acarician un mismo ensueño. Cuando hablaban, el rumor de sus voces se perdía en los rumores de la tarde, y sólo la onda primaveral de sus risas se levantaba armónica bajo la sombra de los clásicos laureles.

Cuando penetré en el salón de la Princesa, ya estaban las luces encendidas. En medio del silencio resonaba llena de gravedad la voz de un Colegial Mayor, que conversaba con las señoras que componían la

with which their eternally youthful voices always appear to accompany thoughts of love. When I leaned over the railing, I felt the breath of spring rising to my face. That old garden of myrtle and laurel was full of heathen charm beneath the setting sun. At the far end, walking down the tortuous paths of a labyrinth, the five sisters appeared, with their skirts full of roses, as in an ancient fable. In the distance, cleaved by numerous lateen sails that looked like amber, stretched the Tyrrhenian Sea. On the beach of golden sand the waves were dying gently, and the sound of the shells with which the fishermen announced their arrival at the shore, and the hoarse chanting of the sea, seemed attuned to the fragrance of that old-fashioned garden in which the five sisters were telling one another their youthful dreams, in the shade of the rosy laurels.

They had sat down on a large stone bench to make up their bouquets. On María Rosario's shoulder sat a dove, and in that naïve event I found the charm and mystery of an allegory. A few village church bells were announcing a feast day, and the church was outlined in the distance atop a green hill, surrounded by cypresses. The procession issued forth and circled the church, and one could make out the images on their carrying platforms, their embroidered mantles gleaming in the sun, and the red parish banners preceding them, fluttering victoriously like liturgical emblems of triumph. The five sisters knelt down on the grass and clasped their rose-filled hands.

The blackbirds were singing on the boughs, and their songs answered one another, linking up into a rhythm as remote as the waves of the sea. The five sisters had taken their seats again. They were weaving their bouquets silently, and amid the purple of the roses their hands fluttered like white doves, and the sunbeams penetrating the foliage trembled on them like fiery, mystical rays. The tritons and mermaids of the fountains burbled their fanciful laughter, and the silvery waters ran with a youthful babble down the mudstained beards of the ancient sea monsters who stooped down to kiss the mermaids they had caught up in their arms. The five sisters rose to return to the palace. They were walking slowly down the paths of the labyrinth, like enchanted princesses caressed by one and the same daydream. When they spoke, the sound of their voices was lost in the sounds of the evening, and only the vernal wave of their laughter rose harmoniously beneath the shade of the classical laurels.

When I entered the princess's salon, the lamps were already lighted. Amid the silence there resounded, full of gravity, the voice of a Collegio member chatting with the ladies who constituted Princess

tertulia de la Princesa Gaetani. El salón era dorado y de un gusto francés, femenino y lujoso. Amorcillos con guirnaldas, ninfas vestidas de encajes, galantes cazadores y venados de enramada cornamenta poblaban la tapicería del muro, y sobre las consolas, en graciosos grupos de porcelana, duques pastores ceñían el florido talle de marquesas aldeanas. Yo me detuve un momento en la puerta. Al verme, las damas que ocupaban el estrado, suspiraron, y el Colegial Mayor se puso en pie:

—Permítame el Señor Capitán que le salude en nombre de todo el Colegio Clementino.

Y me alargó su mano carnosa y blanca, que parecía reclamar la pastoral amatista. Por privilegio pontificio vestía beca de terciopelo, que realzaba su figura prócer y llena de majestad. Era un hombre joven, pero con los cabellos blancos. Tenía los ojos llenos de fuego, la nariz aguileña y la boca de estatua, firme y bien dibujada. La Princesa me lo presentó con un gesto lleno de languidez sentimental:

—Monseñor Antonelli. ¡Un sabio y un santo!

Yo me incliné:

—Sé, Princesa, que los cardenales romanos le consultan las más arduas cuestiones teológicas, y la fama de sus virtudes a todas partes llega . . .

El Colegial interrumpió con su grave voz, reposada y amable:

—No soy más que un filósofo, entendiendo la filosofía como la entendían los antiguos: Amor a la sabiduría.

Después, volviendo a sentarse, continuó:

—¿Habéis visto a Monseñor Gaetani? ¡Qué desgracia! ¡Tan grande como impensada!

Todos guardamos un silencio triste. Dos señoras ancianas, las dos vestidas de seda con noble severidad, interrogaban a un mismo tiempo y con la misma voz:

—¿No hay esperanzas?

La Princesa suspiró:

—No las hay . . . Solamente un milagro.

De nuevo volvió el silencio. En el otro extremo del salón las hijas de la Princesa bordaban un paño de tisú, las cinco sentadas en rueda. Hablaban en voz baja las unas con las otras, y sonreían con las cabezas inclinadas: Sólo María Rosario permanecía silenciosa, y bordaba lentamente como si soñase. Temblaba en las agujas el hilo de oro, y bajo los dedos de las cinco doncellas nacían las rosas y los lirios de la flora celeste que puebla los paños sagrados. De improviso, en medio de aque-

Gaetani's conversation circle. The salon was gilded and was in the French style, feminine and luxurious. Cupids with garlands, nymphs clad in lace, gallant hunters, and deer with branching antlers peopled the wall tapestry; and on the console tables, in graceful porcelain groups, ducal shepherds embraced the flowering waists of village marchionesses. I stopped in the doorway for a moment. On seeing me, the ladies in the drawing room sighed, and the Collegio member stood up:

"I hope the captain will permit me to greet him on behalf of the entire Collegio Clementino."

And he held out to me his fleshy white hand, which seemed to cry out for a prelate's amethyst. By a papal privilege he was wearing a velvet gown that enhanced his lordly, majestic appearance. He was a young man, but his hair was white. His eyes were full of fire, his nose was aquiline, and his lips like a statue's, firm and well outlined. The princess introduced him to me with a gesture redolent of sentimental languor:

"Monsignor Antonelli. A scholar and a saint!"

I bowed:

"I know, princess, that the Roman cardinals consult him on the most difficult questions of theology, and the fame of his virtues extends everywhere . . ."

The ecclesiastic interrupted me with his grave, calm, friendly voice:

"I am merely a philosopher, taking philosophy to mean the same thing that the ancients did: love of wisdom."

Then, sitting down again, he went on:

"Have you seen Monsignor Gaetani? What a misfortune! As great as it is unexpected!"

We all maintained a sad silence. Two elderly ladies, both dressed in silk with noble austerity, asked at the same time, in the same tone of voice:

"Is there no hope?"

The princess sighed:

"None . . . Only a miracle."

Silence returned. At the other end of the salon the princess's daughters were embroidering a lamé fabric, all five seated in a circle. They were talking quietly among themselves and smiling with lowered heads. Only María Rosario remained silent, embroidering slowly as if dreaming. The golden thread was trembling in the needles, and beneath the fingers of the five maidens there blossomed the roses and lilies of the heavenly flora that grows on liturgical vestments. Suddenly, amid that peace, three door-knocker blows rang out. The

lla paz, resonaron tres aldabadas. La Princesa palideció mortalmente: Los demás no hicieron sino mirarse. El Colegial Mayor se puso en pie:

—Permitirán que me retire: No creí que fuese tan tarde . . . ¿Cómo han cerrado ya las puertas?

La Princesa repuso temblando:

—No las han cerrado.

Y las dos ancianas vestidas de seda negra susurraron:

—¡Algún insolente!

Cambiaron entre ellas una mirada tímida, como para infundirse ánimo, y quedaron atentas, con un ligero temblor. Las aldabadas volvían a sonar, pero esta vez era dentro del Palacio Gaetani. Una ráfaga pasó por el salón y apagó algunas luces. La Princesa lanzó un grito. Todos la rodeamos: Ella nos miraba con los labios trémulos y los ojos asustados. Insinuó una voz:

—Cuando murió el Príncipe Filipo, ocurrió esto . . . ¡Y él lo contaba de su padre!

En aquel momento el Señor Polonio apareció en la puerta del salón, y en ella se detuvo. La Princesa incorporóse en el sofá, y se enjugó los ojos: Después, con noble entereza, le interrogó:

—¿Ha muerto?

El mayordomo inclinó la frente:

—¡Ya goza de Dios!

Una onda de gemidos se levantó en el estrado. Las damas rodearon a la Princesa, que con el pañuelo sobre los ojos se desmayaba lánguidamente en el canapé, y el Colegial Mayor se santiguó.

María Rosario, con los ojos arrasados de lágrimas guardaba lentamente sus agujas y su hilo de oro. Yo la veía en el otro extremo del salón, inclinada sobre un menudo y cincelado cofre que sostenía abierto en el regazo: Sin duda rezaba en voz baja, porque sus labios se movían débilmente. En su mejilla temblaba la sombra de las pestañas, y yo sentía que en el fondo de mi alma aquel rostro pálido temblaba con el encanto misterioso y poético que tiembla en el fondo de un lago el rostro de la luna. María Rosario cerró el cofre, y dejando en él la llave de oro, lo puso sobre la alfombra para tomar en brazos a la más niña de sus hermanas, que lloraba asustada. Después se inclinó, besándola. Yo veía cómo la infantil y rubia guedeja de María Nieves desbordaba sobre el brazo de María Rosario, y hallaba en aquel grupo la gracia cándida de esos cuadros antiguos que pintaron los monjes devotos de la Virgen. La niña murmuró:

princess turned deathly pale; the others merely looked at one another. The Collegio member stood up:

"You'll permit me to withdraw. I didn't think it was so late . . . How is it that the doors are already locked?"

Trembling, the princess replied:

"They aren't."

And the two old ladies in black silk whispered:

"Some insolent person!"

The two exchanged a timid glance as if to give each other courage; then they remained attentive, shivering slightly. The knocks were heard again, but this time inside the Gaetani palace. A gust raced through the salon and blew out some of the lamps. The princess uttered a cry. We all encircled her. She looked at us with quivering lips and frightened eyes. A voice suggested:

"When Prince Filippo died, the same thing happened . . . And he used to tell the same story about his father!"

At that moment Master Polonio appeared in the doorway of the salon and remained there. The princess sat up on the sofa and dried her eyes. Then, with noble fortitude, she asked him:

"Has he died?"

The butler lowed his head.

"He's now enjoying the sight of God!"

A wave of moans arose in the drawing room. The ladies stood around the princess, who, her handkerchief over her eyes, was swooning languidly on the settee, and the Collegio member crossed himself.

María Rosario, her eyes brimming with tears, was slowly putting away her needles and her golden thread. I saw her at the other end of the salon bending over a small chiseled case which she held open on her lap. No doubt she was praying in low tones, because her lips were moving feebly. On her cheek the shadow of her lashes was trembling, and I felt that in the depths of my soul that pallid face was trembling with the same mysterious, poetic enchantment with which the face of the moon trembles in the depths of a lake. María Rosario locked the case and, leaving the golden key in it, set it down on the carpet so she could pick up her youngest sister, who was weeping in fright. Then she stooped down, kissing her. I saw how María Nieves's childlike blonde hair flowed down onto María Rosario's arm, and I found in that group the naïve charm of those old pictures painted by monastic devotees of the Virgin. The child murmured:

—¡Tengo sueño!

—¿Quieres que llame a tu doncella para que te acueste?

—Malvina me deja sola. Se figura que estoy durmiendo y se va muy despacio, y cuando quedo sola tengo miedo.

María Rosario alzóse con la niña en brazos, y como una sombra silenciosa y pálida atravesó el salón. Yo acudí presuroso a levantar el cortinaje de la puerta. María Rosario pasó con los ojos bajos, sin mirarme: La niña, en cambio, volvió hacia mí sus claras pupilas llenas de lágrimas, y me dijo con una voz muy tenue:

—Buenas noches, Marqués, hasta mañana.

—Adiós, preciosa.

Y con el alma herida por el desdén que María Rosario me mostrara, volví al estrado, donde la Princesa seguía con el pañuelo sobre los ojos. Las ancianas de su tertulia la rodeaban, y de tiempo en tiempo se volvían aconsejadoras y prudentes para hablar en voz baja con las niñas, que también suspiraban, pero con menos dolor que su madre:

—Hijas mías, debéis hacer que se acueste.

—Hay que disponer los lutos.

—¿Dónde ha ido María Rosario?

El Colegial Mayor también dejaba oír alguna vez su voz grave y amable: Cada palabra suya producía un murmullo de admiración entre las señoras. La verdad es que cuanto manaba en sus labios parecía lleno de ciencia teológica y de unción cristiana: De rato en rato fijaba en mí una mirada rápida y sagaz, y yo comprendía con un estremecimiento, que aquellos ojos negros querían leer en mi alma. Yo era el único que allí permanecía silencioso, y acaso el único que estaba triste. Adivinaba, por primera vez en mi vida, todo el influjo galante de los prelados romanos, y acudía a mi memoria la leyenda de sus fortunas amorosas. Confieso que hubo instantes donde olvidé la ocasión, el sitio y hasta los cabellos blancos que peinaban aquellas nobles damas, y que tuve celos, celos rabiosos del Colegial Mayor. De pronto me estremecí: Hacía un momento que callaban todos, y en medio del silencio, el Colegial se acercaba a mí: Posó familiar su diestra sobre mi hombro, y me dijo:

—Caro Marqués, es preciso enviar un correo a Su Santidad.

Yo me incliné:

—Tenéis razón, Monseñor.

Y él repuso con extremada cortesía:

—Me congratula que seáis del mismo consejo . . . ¡Qué gran desgracia, Marqués!

"I'm sleepy!"

"Do you want me to call your maid to put you to bed?"

"Malvina leaves me all alone. She imagines I'm asleep and she goes away very slowly, and when I'm left alone I get scared."

María Rosario stood up with the child in her arms, and like a silent, pale shadow she crossed the salon. I ran over solicitously to raise the doorway curtain. María Rosario passed through with lowered eyes, not looking at me. On the other hand, the child turned her bright, tear-filled eyes toward me, and said to me in a thread of a voice:

"Good night, marquis. I'll see you tomorrow."

"Good night, dearest."

And with my soul wounded by the disdain María Rosario had shown me, I returned to the drawing room, where the princess still had the handkerchief over her eyes. The old ladies from her conversation circle were around her, and every so often they turned around to offer prudent advice in low tones to the girls, who were also sighing, but not as sorrowfully as their mother:

"My girls, you must make her go to bed."

"The mourning clothes must be laid out."

"Where did María Rosario go?"

At moments the Collegio member also let his grave, pleasant voice be heard. Each word from him elicited a murmur of admiration from the ladies. And indeed, all that issued from his lips seemed full of theological science and Christian unction. From time to time he gave me a rapid, crafty glance, and with a shudder I understood that those dark eyes desired to read my soul. I was the only one there who remained silent, and perhaps the only one who was sad. For the first time in my life I divined the full extent of the gallant influence of Roman prelates, and there came to my memory his reputation for good fortunes in love. I confess that there were instants when I forgot the occasion, the place, and even the whiteness of the hair that those noble ladies combed, and I became jealous, wildly jealous of the Collegio member. All at once I shuddered. There was a moment when everyone was silent, and amid the silence, the Collegio member came up to me. Familiarly, he laid his right hand on my shoulder and said:

"My dear marquis, a courier must be sent to His Holiness."

I bowed:

"You are right, Monsignor."

And he replied with the utmost courtesy:

"I am pleased that you are of the same mind . . . What a great misfortune, marquis!"

—¡Muy grande, Monseñor!

Nos miramos de hito en hito, con un profundo convencimiento de que fingíamos por igual, y nos separamos. El Colegial Mayor volvió al lado de la Princesa, y yo salí del salón para escribir al Cardenal Camarlengo, que lo era entonces Monseñor Sassoferrato.

¡María Rosario, en aquella hora fortuita, tal vez estaba velando el cadáver de Monseñor Gaetani! Tuve este pensamiento al entrar en la biblioteca, llena de silencio y de sombras. Vino del mundo lejano, y pasó sobre mi alma como soplo de aire sobre un lago de misterio. Sentí en las sienes el frío de unas manos mortales, y, estremecido, me puse en pie. Quedó abandonado sobre la mesa el pliego de papel, donde solamente había trazado la cruz, y dirigí mis pasos hacia la cámara mortuoria. El olor de la cera llenaba el Palacio. Criados silenciosos velaban en los largos corredores, y en la antecámara paseaban dos familiares, que me saludaron con una inclinación de cabeza. Sólo se oía el rumor de sus pisadas y el chisporroteo de los cirios que ardían en la alcoba.

Yo llegué hasta la puerta y me detuve: Monseñor Gaetani yacía rígido en su lecho, amortajado con hábito franciscano: En las manos yertas sostenía una cruz de plata, y sobre su rostro marfileño, la llama de los cirios tan pronto ponía un resplandor como una sombra. Allá, en el fondo de la estancia, rezaba María Rosario: Yo permanecí un momento mirándola: Ella levantó los ojos, se santiguó tres veces, besó la cruz de sus dedos, y poniéndose en pie vino hacia la puerta:

—¿Marqués, queda mi madre en el salón?

—Allí la dejé . . .

—Es preciso que descanse, porque ya lleva así dos noches . . . ¡Adiós, Marqués!

—¿No queréis que os acompañe?

Ella se volvió:

—Acompañadme, sí . . . La verdad es que María Nieves me ha contagiado su miedo . . .

Atravesamos la antecámara. Los familiares detuvieron un momento el silencioso pasear, y sus ojos inquisidores nos siguieron hasta la puerta. Salimos al corredor que estaba solo, y sin poder dominarme estreché una mano de María Rosario y quise besarla, pero ella la retiró con vivo enojo:

"Very great, Monsignor!"

We stared at each other, thoroughly convinced that we were both pretending, and we parted. The Collegio member returned to the princess's side, and I left the salon in order to write to the Cardinal Camerlingo,[6] who at that time was Monsignor Sassoferrato.

In that chance hour, María Rosario may have been keeping vigil beside Monsignor Gaetani's body! That was what I was thinking when I entered the silence- and shadow-filled library. Coming from a distant world, that thought passed over my soul like a breath of air over a lake of mystery. I felt in my temples the chill of dying hands and with a shudder I stood up. The sheet of paper, on which I had merely drawn the opening cross, remained abandoned on the table, and I directed my steps toward the deathbed chamber. The smell of wax filled the palace. Silent servants were watching in the long corridors, and in the anteroom two familiars were walking; they greeted me with a nod. All that could be heard was the sound of their steps and the sizzling of the tapers burning in the bedroom.

I arrived as far as the door and I stopped. Monsignor Gaetani was lying rigid on his bed, shrouded in a Franciscan habit. In his stiff hands he held a silver cross, and on his ivory face the taper light shed a glow at one moment and cast a shadow at another. There, at the far end of the room, María Rosario was praying. I remained gazing at her for a moment. She raised her eyes, crossed herself three times, kissed the cross which her fingers formed, stood up, and came to the door:

"Marquis, is my mother still in the salon?"

"She was there when I left . . ."

"She must get some rest, because she's been this way for two nights now . . . Good night, marquis!"

"You don't want me to accompany you?"

She turned around:

"Do accompany me, yes . . . To tell the truth, I've caught María Nieves's fear . . ."

We crossed the anteroom. For a moment the familiars ceased their silent pacing, and their inquisitorial eyes followed us to the door. We emerged into the corridor, which was empty, and, unable to control myself, I pressed one of María Rosario's hands and tried to kiss it, but she withdrew it in high indignation:

---

6. In charge of the business affairs of the college of cardinals.

—¿Qué hacéis?

—¡Que os adoro! ¡Que os adoro!

Asustada, huyó por el largo corredor. Yo la seguí:

—¡Os adoro! ¡Os adoro!

Mi aliento casi rozaba su nuca, que era blanca como la de una estatua y exhalaba no sé qué aroma de flor y de doncella.

—¡Os adoro! ¡Os adoro!

Ella suspiró con angustia:

—¡Dejadme! ¡Por favor, dejadme!

Y sin volver la cabeza, azorada, trémula, huía por el corredor. Sin aliento y sin fuerzas se detuvo en la puerta del salón. Yo todavía murmuré a su oído:

—¡Os adoro! ¡Os adoro!

María Rosario se pasó la mano por los ojos y entró. Yo entré detrás atusándome el mostacho. María Rosario se detuvo bajo la lámpara y me miró con ojos asustados, enrojeciendo de pronto: Luego quedó pálida, pálida como la muerte. Vacilando, se acercó a sus hermanas, y tomó asiento entre ellas, que se inclinaron en sus sillas para interrogarla: Apenas respondía. Se hablaban en voz baja con tímida mesura, y en los momentos de silencio oíase el péndulo de un reloj. Poco a poco había ido menguando la tertulia: Solamente quedaban aquellas dos señoras de los cabellos blancos y los vestidos de gro negro. Ya cerca de medianoche la Princesa consintió en retirarse a descansar, pero sus hijas continuaron en el salón velando hasta el día, acompañadas por las dos señoras que contaban historias de su juventud. Recuerdos de antiguas modas femeninas y de las guerras de Bonaparte. Yo escuchaba distraído, y desde el fondo de un sillón, oculto en la sombra, contemplaba a María Rosario: Parecía sumida en un ensueño: Su boca, pálida de ideales nostalgias, permanecía anhelante, como si hablase con las almas invisibles, y sus ojos inmóviles, abiertos sobre el infinito, miraban sin ver. Al contemplarla, yo sentía que en mi corazón se levantaba el amor, ardiente y trémulo como una llama mística. Todas mis pasiones se purificaban en aquel fuego sagrado y aromaban como gomas de Arabia. ¡Han pasado muchos años y todavía el recuerdo me hace suspirar!

Ya cerca del amanecer me retiré a la biblioteca. Era forzoso escribir al Cardenal Camarlengo, y decidí hacerlo en aquellas horas de monótona tristeza, cuando todas las campanas de Ligura se despertaban tocando a muerto, y prestes y arciprestes con rezo latino en-

"What are you doing?"

"I adore you! I adore you!"

She fled in fright down the long corridor. I followed her:

"I adore you! I adore you!"

My breath was nearly grazing her neck, which was as white as a statue's and emitted a sort of mingled fragrance of flower and maiden.

"I adore you! I adore you!"

She sighed in anguish:

"Let me alone! Please let me alone!"

And without turning her head, flustered, timorous, she fled down the corridor. Breathless, her strength gone, she stopped at the door to the salon. I still whispered in her ear:

"I adore you! I adore you!"

María Rosario passed her hand over her eyes and went in. I went in after her, smoothing my mustache. María Rosario halted beneath the lamp and looked at me with frightened eyes, suddenly blushing. Then she turned pale, pale as death. Waveringly she approached her sisters and sat down in their midst as they bent forward on their chairs to question her. She could scarcely reply. They spoke to one another in low tones with shy restraint, and at moments of silence one could hear the pendulum of a clock. The conversation circle had gradually dwindled. The only ones left were those two white-haired ladies dressed in black grosgrain. Now that it was nearly midnight, the princess consented to withdraw and take some rest, but her daughters remained in the salon, keeping vigil until daylight, accompanied by the two ladies, who told them stories from their youth. Recollections of bygone women's fashions and of the Napoleonic wars. I listened absentmindedly, and from the depths of an armchair, hidden in the shadow, I observed María Rosario. She seemed to be immersed in a daydream. Her lips, pallid with imaginary longings, remained avid, as if she were speaking to invisible souls, and her unmoving eyes, open onto infinity, gazed without seeing. When I studied her, I felt love stirring in my heart, ardent and trembling as a mystic flame. All my passions were being purified in that sacred fire and becoming fragrant as Arabian spices. Many years have gone by and that memory still makes me sigh!

It was nearly dawn when I withdrew to the library. It was imperative to write to the Cardinal Camerlingo, and I resolved to do so during those hours of monotonous sadness when every church bell in Ligura was awakening in a funerary toll, and priests and archpriests,

comendaban a Dios el alma del difunto Obispo de Betulia. En mi carta, dile a Monseñor Sassoferrato cuenta de todo muy extensamente, y luego de haber lacrado y puesto los cinco sellos con las armas pontificias, llamé al mayordomo y le entregué el pliego para que sin pérdida de momento un correo lo llevase a Roma. Hecho esto me dirigí al oratorio de la Princesa, donde sin intervalo se sucedían las misas desde antes de rayar el sol. Primero habían celebrado los familiares que velaran el cadáver de Monseñor Gaetani, después los capellanes de la casa, y luego algún obeso colegial mayor que llegaba apresurado y jadeante. La Princesa había mandado franquear las puertas del Palacio, y a lo largo de los corredores sentíase el sordo murmullo del pueblo que entraba a visitar el cadáver. Los criados vigilaban en las antesalas, y los acólitos pasaban y repasaban con su ropón rojo y su roquete blanco, metiéndose a empujones por entre los devotos.

Al entrar en el oratorio, mi corazón palpitó. Allí estaba María Rosario, y cercano a ella tuve la suerte de oír misa. Recibida la bendición, me adelanté a saludarla. Ella me respondió temblando: También mi corazón temblaba, pero los ojos de María Rosario no podían verlo. Yo hubiérale rogado que pusiese su mano sobre mi pecho, pero temí que desoyese mi ruego. Aquella niña era cruel como todas las santas que tremolan en la tersa diestra la palma virginal. Confieso que yo tengo predilección por aquellas otras que primero han sido grandes pecadoras. Desgraciadamente María Rosario nunca quiso comprender que era su destino mucho menos bello que el de María de Magdala. La pobre no sabía que lo mejor de la santidad son las tentaciones. Quise ofrecerle agua bendita, y con galante apresuramiento me adelanté a tomarla: María Rosario tocó apenas mis dedos, y haciendo la señal de la cruz, salió del oratorio. Salí detrás, y pude verla un momento en el fondo tenebroso del corredor, hablando con el mayordomo. Al parecer le daba órdenes en voz baja: Volvió la cabeza, y viendo que me acercaba, enrojeció vivamente. El mayordomo exclamó:

—¡Aquí está el Señor Marqués!

Y luego, dirigiéndose a mí con una profunda reverencia, continuó:

—Excelencia, perdonad que os moleste, pero decid si estáis quejoso de mí. ¿He cometido con vos alguna falta, acaso algún olvido . . . ?

María Rosario le interrumpió con enojo:

—Callad, Polonio.

El melifluo mayordomo pareció consternado:

in Latin prayers, were commending to God the soul of the late bishop
of Betulia. In my letter I related everything to Monsignor Sassoferrato
in great detail, and after applying wax and imprinting the five seals
with the papal escutcheon, I summoned the butler and handed him
the message, so that, without wasting a moment, a courier could take
it to Rome. Next, I headed for the princess's chapel, where one mass
had followed another uninterruptedly since before sunrise. The first
celebrants had been the familiars who had kept vigil by Monsignor
Gaetani's body, then the house chaplains, and then one or another
obese Collegio member, arriving hastily and panting. The princess
had ordered the palace to be opened to the public, and all along the
corridors could be heard the muffled murmuring of the townspeople
who had come to see the body. The servants kept watch in the an-
techambers, and the acolytes passed to and fro in their red gowns and
white rochets, elbowing their way into the pious crowd.

As I entered the chapel, my heart palpitated. There was María
Rosario, and I was lucky enough to hear mass in her proximity. After receiving the benediction, I went over to greet her. She trembled as she
answered me. My heart was trembling, too, but María Rosario's eyes
couldn't see that. I would have asked her to place her hand on my
bosom, but I was afraid she would fail to grant my request. That girl was
as cruel as all those female saints who wave the palm of virginity in their
smooth right hand. I confess that my preference is for those other female
saints who were formerly great sinners. Unfortunately María Rosario
never wanted to understand that her destiny was much less beautiful
than that of Mary of Magdala. The poor girl was unaware that the best
thing about sainthood is its temptations. I tried to offer her holy water,
and with gallant solicitousness I arrived at the stoup first: María Rosario
barely touched my fingers and, making the sign of the cross, left the
chapel. I left after her and I was able to see her for a moment at the
shadowy far end of the corridor, speaking with the butler. She seemed to
be giving him orders in a low tone. She turned her head and, seeing me
drawing near, she blushed brightly. The butler exclaimed:

"Here is the marquis!"

And then, addressing me with a low bow, he went on:

"Excellency, forgive me for troubling you, but tell me if you are an-
noyed with me. Have I committed any fault with regard to you, perhaps some negligence? . . ."

María Rosario interrupted him angrily:

"Be quiet, Polonio!"

The eloquent butler seemed dismayed:

—¿Qué hice yo para merecer . . . ?

—Os digo que calléis.

—Y os obedezco, pero como me reprocháis haber descuidado el servicio del Señor Marqués . . .

María Rosario, con las mejillas llameantes y la voz timbrada de cólera y de lágrimas, volvió a interrumpir:

—Os mando que calléis. Son insoportables vuestras explicaciones.

—¿Qué hice yo, cándida paloma, qué hice yo?

María Rosario, con un poco más de indulgencia, murmuró:

—¡Basta . . . ! ¡Basta . . . ! Perdonad, Marqués.

Y haciéndome una leve cortesía, se alejó. El mayordomo quedóse en medio del corredor con las manos en la cabeza y los ojos llorosos:

—Hubiérame tratado así una de sus hermanas, y me hubiera reído . . . La más pequeña no ignora que es princesina. No, no me hubiera reído, porque son mis señoras . . . Pero ella, ella que jamás ha reñido con nadie, venir a reñir hoy con este pobre viejo . . . ! Y qué injustamente, qué injustamente!

Yo le pregunté con una emoción para mí desconocida hasta entonces:

—¿Es la mejor de sus hermanas?

—Y la mejor de las criaturas. Esa niña ha sido engendrada por los ángeles . . .

Y el Señor Polonio, enternecido, comenzó un largo relato de las virtudes que adornaban el alma de aquella doncella hija de príncipes, y era el relato del viejo mayordomo ingenuo y sencillo, como los que pueblan la Leyenda Dorada.

¡Llegaban por el cadáver de Monseñor . . . ! Y el mayordomo partióse de mi lado muy afligido y presuroso. Todas las campanas de la histórica ciudad doblaban a un tiempo. Oíase el canto latino de los clérigos resonando bajo el pórtico del Palacio, y el murmullo de la gente que llenaba la plaza. Cuatro colegiales mayores bajaron en hombros el féretro, y el duelo se puso en marcha. Monseñor Antonelli me hizo sitio a su derecha, y con humildad, que me pareció estudiada, comenzó a dolerse de lo mucho que con la muerte de aquel santo y de aquel sabio perdía el Colegio Clementino. Yo a todo asentía con un vago gesto, y disimuladamente miraba a las ventanas llenas de mujeres. Monseñor tardó poco en advertirlo, y me dijo con una sonrisa tan amable como sagaz:

"What have I done to deserve . . . ?"

"I say, be quiet!"

"And I obey you, but since you reproach me for having served the marquis inadequately . . ."

María Rosario, her cheeks aflame and her voice indicative of wrath and tears, interrupted him again:

"I order you to be quiet! Your explanations are unbearable."

"What have I done, my white dove, what have I done?"

María Rosario, somewhat more indulgently, whispered:

"Enough! Enough! Forgive us, marquis!"

And curtseying to me lightly, she moved away. The butler remained in the middle of the corridor, his hands on his head and tears in his eyes:

"If one of her sisters had treated me like that, I would just have laughed . . . The littlest one is well aware that she's a princess. No, I wouldn't have laughed, because they're my young ladies . . . But she, she who has never chided anyone—that *she* should today chide this poor old man . . . And so unfairly, so unfairly!"

I asked him with an emotion unfamiliar to me earlier:

"Is she the kindest of the sisters?"

"And the kindest of creatures. That girl was begotten by the angels . . ."

And Master Polonio, touched, began a long recitation of the virtues which adorned the soul of that maiden, daughter of princes; and the narrative of the old butler was as naïve and unsophisticated as those that appear in the *Golden Legend*.

People were coming for Monsignor's body . . . ! And the butler, in great affliction and haste, left me there. All the church bells in the historic city were tolling at once. One could hear the Latin chants of the ecclesiastics echoing beneath the portico of the palace, and the murmuring of the townspeople who filled the square. Four Collegio members carried down the bier on their shoulders, and the funeral procession set out. Monsignor Antonelli made a place for me at his right and, with what seemed to me a studied humility, he began to lament the great loss to the Collegio Clementino caused by the death of that saint and scholar. I agreed to everything with a vague gesture, and kept looking furtively at the windows, which were crowded with women. Monsignor noticed this before very long, and said to me with a smile as crafty as it was friendly:

—Sin duda no conocéis nuestra ciudad.

—No, Monseñor.

—Si permanecéis algún tiempo entre nosotros y queréis conocerla, yo me ofrezco a ser vuestro guía. ¡Está llena de riquezas artísticas!

—Gracias, Monseñor.

Seguimos en silencio. El son de las campanas llenaba el aire, y el grave cántico de los clérigos parecía reposar en la tierra, donde todo es polvo y podredumbre. Jaculatorias, misereres, responsos caían sobre el féretro como el agua bendita del hisopo. Encima de nuestras cabezas las campanas seguían siempre sonando, y el sol, un sol abrileño, joven y rubio como un mancebo, brillaba en las vestiduras sagradas, en la seda de los pendones y en las cruces parroquiales con un alarde de poder pagano.

Atravesamos casi toda la ciudad. Monseñor había dispuesto que se diese tierra a su cuerpo en el Convento de los Franciscanos, donde hacía más de cuatro siglos tenían enterramiento los Príncipes Gaetani. Una tradición piadosa, dice que el Santo de Asís fundó el Convento de Ligura, y que vivió allí algún tiempo. Todavía florece en el huerto el viejo rosal que se cubría de rosas en todas las ocasiones que visitaba aquella fundación el Divino Francisco. Llegamos entre dobles de campanas. En la puerta de la iglesia, alumbrándose con cirios, esperaba la Comunidad dividida en dos largas hileras. Primero los novicios, pálidos, ingenuos, demacrados: Después los profesos, sombríos, torturados, penitentes. Todos rezaban con la vista baja y sobre las sandalias los cirios lloraban gota a gota su cera amarilla.

Dijéronse muchas misas, cantóse un largo entierro, y el ataúd bajó al sepulcro que esperaba abierto desde el amanecer. Cayó la losa encima, y un colegial me buscó con deferencia cortesana, para llevarme a la sacristía. Los frailes seguían murmurando sus responsos, y la iglesia iba quedando en soledad y en silencio. En la sacristía saludé a muchos sabios y venerables teólogos que me edificaron con sus pláticas. Luego vino el Prior, un anciano de blanca barba, que había vivido largos años en los Santos Lugares. Me saludó con dulzura evangélica, y haciéndome sentar a su lado comenzó a preguntarme por la salud de Su Santidad. Los graves teólogos hicieron corro para escuchar mis nuevas, y como era muy poco lo que podía decirles, tuve que inventar en honor suyo toda una leyenda piadosa y milagrera: ¡Su Santidad recobrando la lozanía juvenil por medio de una reliquia! El Prior con el rostro resplandeciente de fe, me preguntó:

—¿De qué Santo era, hijo mío?

—De un Santo de mi familia.

"No doubt you aren't familiar with our city."

"No, Monsignor."

"If you remain with us for any time and wish to get to know it, I volunteer to be your guide. It's full of artistic treasures!"

"Thank you, Monsignor."

We proceeded in silence. The sound of the bells filled the air, and the solemn chanting of the priests seemed to be hugging the ground, where all is dust and decay. Short prayers, misereres, and prayers for the dead rained onto the bier like the holy water of the aspergillum. Over our heads the bells kept tolling ceaselessly, and the sun, an April sun, young and blond as a lad, gleamed on the holy vestments, on the silk of the banners, and on the parish crosses with a bold display of pagan power.

We crossed almost the whole town. Monsignor had arranged for his body to be interred in the Franciscan monastery, where the Princes Gaetani had been buried for over four centuries. A pious tradition recounts that the friary in Ligura was founded by the saint of Assisi himself, and that he dwelt there for some time. Still blossoming in the garden is the old rosebush that used to be covered with roses every time that the divine Francis visited that house he had founded. We arrived amid the tolling of bells. At the church door, lighting their way with tapers, the community of friars was waiting in two long files. First the novices, pale, naïve, emaciated. Next, those who had taken vows, somber, tortured, penitent. They were all praying with downcast eyes, and drop by drop the tapers were weeping their yellow wax onto the men's sandals.

Many masses were read, a long funeral service was sung, and the coffin descended to the grave which had been lying open since dawn. The flagstone dropped on top of it, and a Collegio member sought me out with a courtier's deference, to take me to the sacristy. The friars kept muttering their prayers for the dead, and the church gradually became empty and silent. In the sacristy I greeted many learned and venerable theologians who edified me with their discourse. Then the prior arrived, an elderly man with a white beard who had lived for many years in the Holy Land. He greeted me with evangelical gentleness and, having me sit beside him, began inquiring of me as to His Holiness's health. The grave theologians gathered around in a circle to listen to my report, and since there was very little I could tell them, I had to invent an entire pious, miraculous legend in their honor. His Holiness regaining the vigor of his youth by means of a relic! The prior, his face beaming with faith, asked me:

"What saint's was it, my son?"

"It belonged to a saint from my family."

Todos se inclinaron como si yo fuese el Santo. El temblor de un rezo pasó por las luengas barbas, que salían del misterio de las capuchas, y en aquel momento yo sentí el deseo de arrodillarme y besar la mano del Prior. Aquella mano que sobre todos mis pecados podía hacer la cruz: Ego te Absolvo.

Cuando volví al Palacio Gaetani, hallé a María Rosario en la puerta de la capilla repartiendo limosnas entre una corte de mendigos que alargaban las manos escuálidas bajo los rotos mantos. María Rosario era una figura ideal que me hizo recordar aquellas santas hijas de príncipes y de reyes: doncellas de soberana hermosura, que con sus manos delicadas curaban a los leprosos. El alma de aquella niña encendíase con el mismo anhelo de santidad. A una vieja encorvada le decía:

—¿Cómo está tu marido, Liberata?

—¡Siempre lo mismo, señorina . . . ! ¡Siempre lo mismo!

Y después de recoger su limosna y de besarla, retirábase la vieja salmodiando bendiciones, temblona sobre su báculo. María Rosario la miraba un momento, y luego sus ojos compasivos se tornaban hacia otra mendiga que daba el pecho a un niño escuálido, envuelto en el jirón de un manto:

—¿Es tuyo ese niño, Paula?

—No, Princesina: Era de una curmana que se ha muerto: Tres ha dejado la pobre, éste es el más pequeño.

—¿Y tú lo has recogido?

—¡La madre me lo recomendó al morir!

—¿Y qué es de los otros dos?

—Por esas calles andan. El uno tiene cinco años, el otro siete. ¡Pena da mirarlos, desnudos como ángeles del Cielo!

María Rosario tomó en brazos al niño, y lo besó con dos lágrimas en los ojos. Al entregárselo a la mendiga le dijo:

—Vuelve esta tarde y pregunta por el Señor Polonio.

—¡Gracias, mi señorina!

Un murmullo, ardiente como una oración, entreabrió las bocas renegridas y tristes de aquellos mendigos:

—¡La pobre madre se lo agradecerá en el Cielo!

María Rosario continuó:

Everyone bowed as if I were the saint. The tremor of a prayer ran through their long beards, which emerged from the mystery of their cowls, and at that moment I felt an urge to kneel down and kiss the prior's hand—that hand which was able to make the sign of the cross over all my sins: "I absolve you."

When I returned to the Gaetani palace, I found María Rosario in the chapel doorway, distributing alms to an assembly of beggars who held out their scrawny hands from under their tattered capes. María Rosario was a symbolic figure reminding me of those saintly daughters of princes and kings, damsels of sovereign beauty, who cured lepers with their delicate hands. That girl's soul was kindled with the same longing for sainthood. To a stooped old woman she was saying:

"How is your husband, Liberata?"

"The same as ever, signorina . . . ! The same as ever!"

And after receiving her alms and kissing her, the old woman withdrew, mouthing blessings, shaky on her staff. María Rosario watched her for a moment, then her compassionate eyes turned toward another beggar woman who was nursing a skinny child wrapped in the torn shred of a cape:

"Is that boy yours, Paula?"

"No, princess. He belonged to a first cousin[7] of mine who died. The poor woman left behind three; this is the youngest."

"And you took him in?"

"His mother entrusted him to me when she was dying!"

"And what about the other two?"

"They wander the streets. One is five, the other seven. It's heartbreaking to see them, naked as cherubs in heaven!"

María Rosario took the child in her arms and kissed him, with two tears in her eyes. When she handed him back to the beggar woman, she said:

"Come back this afternoon and ask for Master Polonio."

"Thank you, signorina!"

A murmur, ardent as a prayer, parted the blackened, sad lips of those beggars:

"The poor mother will thank you for it in heaven!"

María Rosario continued:

---

7. *Curmana* (for Castilian *prima* [*hermana*]) is a prime example of a Galicianism in Valle-Inclán's writing. Here he is conveying an Italian peasant's speech by means of a rural term from his own native region.

—Y si encuentras a los otros dos pequeños, tráelos también contigo.

—Los otros, hoy no sé dónde poder hallarlos, mi Princesina.

Un viejo de calva sien y luenga barba nevada, sereno y evangélico en su pobreza, se adelantó gravemente:

—Los otros, aunque cativo, tienen también amparo. Los ha recogido Barberina la Prisca, una viuda lavandera que también a mí me tiene recogido.

Y el viejo, que insensiblemente había ido algunos pasos hacia adelante, retrocedió tentando en el suelo con el báculo, y en el aire con una mano, porque era ciego. María Rosario lloraba en silencio, y resplandecía hermosa y cándida como una Madona, en medio de la sórdida corte de mendigos que se acercaban de rodillas para besarle las manos. Aquellas cabezas humildes, demacradas, miserables, tenían una expresión de amor. Yo recordé entonces los antiguos cuadros, vistos tantas veces en un antiguo monasterio de la Umbría, tablas prerrafaélicas, que pintó en el retiro de su celda un monje desconocido, enamorado de los ingenuos milagros que florecen la leyenda de la reina de Turingia.

María Rosario también tenía una hermosa leyenda, y los lirios blancos de la caridad también la aromaban. Vivía en el Palacio como en un convento. Cuando bajaba al jardín traía la falda llena de espliego que esparcía entre sus vestidos, y cuando sus manos se aplicaban a una labor monjil, su mente soñaba sueños de santidad. Eran sueños albos como las parábolas de Jesús, y el pensamiento acariciaba los sueños, como la mano acaricia el suave y tibio plumaje de las palomas familiares. María Rosario hubiera querido convertir el Palacio en albergue donde se recogiese la procesión de viejos y lisiados, de huérfanos y locos que llenaba la capilla pidiendo limosna y salmodiando padrenuestros. Suspiraba recordando la historia de aquellas santas princesas que acogían en sus castillos a los peregrinos que volvían de Jerusalén. También ella era santa y princesa. Sus días se deslizaban como esos arroyos silenciosos que parecen llevar dormido en su fondo el cielo que reflejan: Reza y borda en el silencio de las grandes salas desiertas y melancólicas: Tiemblan las oraciones en sus labios, tiembla en sus dedos la aguja que enhebra el hilo de oro, y en el paño de tisú florecen las rosas y los lirios que pueblan los mantos sagrados. Y después del día lleno de quehaceres humildes, silenciosos, cristianos, por las noches se arrodilla en su alcoba, y reza con fe ingenua al Niño

"And if you run across the other two little ones, bring them along, too."
"I don't know where I can find the others today, princess."
An old man with bald temples and a long snowy beard, serene and evangelical in his poverty, advanced solemnly:
"The others have a shelter, too, even if a poor one. They were taken in by Barberina La Prisca, a widowed washerwoman, who has taken me in, as well."
And the old man, who had imperceptibly taken a few steps forward, retreated, tapping on the ground with his stick and groping in the air with his free hand, because he was blind. María Rosario was weeping silently, and she glowed, beautiful and candid as a Madonna, amid the squalid crowd of beggars who were approaching on their knees to kiss her hands. Those humble, emaciated, poverty-stricken faces bore a loving expression. That reminded me of the antique paintings I had so often viewed in an old monastery in Umbria, pictures from before the time of Raphael, painted in the seclusion of his cell by an unknown monk who was enamored of the naïve miracles that adorn the legend of the queen of Thuringia.[8]

María Rosario, too, had a beautiful reputation, and the white lilies of charity made *her* fragrant, too. She lived in her palace as if in a convent. When she descended to the garden, she filled her skirt with lavender, which she scattered among her clothes; and when her hands undertook some nunlike needlework, her mind dreamt dreams of sainthood. Those dreams were as white as the parables of Jesus, and her thoughts caressed her dreams as a hand caresses the soft, warm feathers of domestic doves. María Rosario would have liked to convert the palace into a hostel in which to take in the procession of the aged and halt, orphans and madmen, which filled the chapel begging for alms and reciting Our Father's. She would sigh when recollecting the story of those saintly princesses who welcomed to their castles the pilgrims returning from Jerusalem. She, too, was saintly and a princess. Her days flowed by like those quiet streams that seem to guard in their beds the dormant reflection of the sky above them. She prays and embroiders in the silence of the great halls, empty and melancholy. The prayers tremble on her lips, the needle holding the golden thread trembles in her fingers, and on the lamé fabric bloom the roses and lilies which grow on sacred vestments. And at the end of a day filled with humble, silent, Christian chores, at night she kneels in her bedroom and prays with naïve faith to the Christ Child who

---

8. This no doubt refers to Saint Elizabeth of Hungary (1207–1231), daughter of a Hungarian king and wife of the Landgrave of Thuringia in Germany.

Jesús, que resplandece bajo un fanal, vestido con alba de seda recamada de lentejuelas y abalorios. La paz familiar se levanta como una alondra del nido de su pecho, y revolotea por todo el Palacio, y canta sobre las puertas, a la entrada de las grandes salas. María Rosario fue el único amor de mi vida. Han pasado muchos años, y al recordarla ahora todavía se llenan de lágrimas mis ojos áridos, ya casi ciegos.

Quedaban todavía los olores de la cera en el Palacio. La Princesa, tendida en el canapé de su tocador, se dolía de la jaqueca. Sus hijas, vestidas de luto, hablaban en voz baja, y de tiempo en tiempo entraba o salía sin ruido alguna de ellas. En medio de un gran silencio, la Princesa incorporóse lánguidamente, volviendo hacia mí el rostro todavía hermoso, que parecía más blanco bajo una toca de negro encaje:

—¿Xavier, tú cuándo tienes que volver a Roma?

Yo me estremecí:

—Mañana, señora.

Y miré a María Rosario, que bajó la cabeza y se puso encendida como una rosa. La Princesa, sin reparar en ello, apoyó la frente en la mano, una mano evocación de aquellas que en los retratos antiguos sostienen a veces una flor, y a veces un pañolito de encaje: En tan bella actitud suspiró largamente, y volvió a interrogarme:

—¿Por qué mañana?

—Porque ha terminado mi misión, señora.

—¿Y no puedes quedarte algunos días más con nosotras?

—Necesitaría un permiso.

—Pues yo escribiré hoy mismo a Roma.

Miré disimuladamente a María Rosario: Sus hermosos ojos negros me contemplaban asustados, y su boca intensamente pálida, que parecía entreabierta por el anhelo de un suspiro, temblaba. En aquel momento, su madre volvió la cabeza hacia donde ella estaba:

—María Rosario.

—Señora.

—Acuérdate de escribir en mi nombre a Monseñor Sassoferrato. Yo firmaré la carta.

María Rosario, siempre ruborosa, repuso con aquella serena dulzura que era como un aroma:

—¿Queréis que escriba ahora?

—Como te parezca, hija.

María Rosario se puso en pie.

gleams below a lamp, dressed in a silk alb embroidered with spangles and glass beads. The peace of the household ascends like a lark from the nest of her bosom, and flutters throughout the palace, singing over the doorways, at the entrance to the great halls. María Rosario was the one and only love of my life. Many years have gone by, but when I remember her now, tears still fill my dry, nearly blind eyes.

The smell of wax still lingered in the palace. The princess, stretched out on the settee in her dressing room, was complaining of headache. Her daughters, dressed in mourning, were talking in low tones, and every so often one or another of them would come in or go out noiselessly. Amid a great silence, the princess sat up languidly, turning in my direction that still beautiful face of hers, which seemed even whiter beneath a black lace cap:

"Xavier, when must you return to Rome?"

I shuddered:

"Tomorrow, madam."

And I looked at María Rosario, who bowed her head and turned red as a rose. Not noticing this, the princess leaned her forehead on her hand, a hand reminiscent of those which in old portraits sometimes hold a flower, sometimes a small lace handkerchief. In that lovely pose she gave a long sigh, and questioned me again:

"Why tomorrow?"

"Because my mission is accomplished, madam."

"And can't you stay with us a few more days?"

"I'd need authorization."

"In that case I'll write to Rome this very day."

I glanced furtively at María Rosario. Her beautiful dark eyes were observing me in fright, and her intensely pale lips, seemingly parted by the passage of a sigh, were quivering. At that moment, her mother turned to face in her direction:

"María Rosario!"

"Madam?"

"Remember to write to Monsignor Sassoferrato on my behalf. I'll sign the letter."

María Rosario, still blushing, replied with that serene sweetness which was like a fragrance:

"Do you want me to write it now?"

"Just as you wish, daughter."

María Rosario rose to her feet.

—¿Y qué debo de decirle a Monseñor?

—Le notificas nuestra desgracia, y añades que vivimos muy solas, y que esperamos de su bondad un permiso para retener a nuestro lado por algún tiempo al Marqués de Bradomín.

María Rosario se dirigió hacia la puerta: Tuvo que pasar por mi lado y aprovechando audazmente la ocasión, le dije en voz baja:

—¡Me quedo, porque os adoro!

Fingió no haberme oído, y salió. Volvíme entonces hacia la Princesa, que me miraba con una sombra de afán, y le pregunté aparentando indiferencia:

—¿Cuándo toma el velo María Rosario?

—No está designado el día.

—La muerte de Monseñor Gaetani, acaso lo retardará.

—¿Por qué?

—Porque ha de ser un nuevo disgusto para vos.

—No soy egoísta. Comprendo que mi hija será feliz en el convento, mucho más feliz que a mi lado, y me resigno.

—¿Es muy antigua la vocación de María Rosario?

—Desde niña.

—¿Y no ha tenido veleidades?

—¡Jamás!

Yo me atusé el bigote con la mano un poco trémula:

—Es una vocación de Santa.

—Sí, de Santa . . . Te advierto que no sería la primera en nuestra familia. Santa Margarita de Ligura, Abadesa de Fiesoli, era hija de un Príncipe Gaetani. Su cuerpo se conserva en la capilla del Palacio, y después de cuatrocientos años está como si acabase de expirar: Parece dormida. ¿Tú no bajaste a la cripta?

—No, señora.

—Pues es preciso que bajes un día.

Quedamos en silencio. La Princesa volvió a suspirar llevándose las manos a la frente: Sus hijas, allá en el fondo de la estancia, se hablaban en voz baja. Yo las miraba sonriendo y ellas me respondían en idéntica forma, con cierta alegría infantil y burlona que contrastaba con sus negros vestidos de duelo. Empezaba a decaer la tarde, y la Princesa mandó abrir una ventana que daba sobre el jardín:

—¡Me marea el olor de esas rosas, hijas mías!

Y señalaba los floreros que estaban sobre el tocador. Abierta la ventana, una ligera brisa entró en la estancia. Era alegre, perfumada y gentil como un mensaje de la Primavera: Sus alas invisibles alboro-

"And what am I to say to Monsignor?"

"You will inform him of our misfortune, and you will add that we live in great seclusion, and that we hope he will be so kind as to allow us to keep the Marquis of Bradomín with us for some time."

María Rosario headed for the door. She had to pass next to me, and boldly taking advantage of the opportunity, I said to her in low tones:

"I'm staying because I adore you!"

She pretended not to have heard me, and she went out. Then I turned to the princess, who was looking at me with a tinge of anxiety, and, feigning indifference, I asked her:

"When is María Rosario to take the veil?"

"No day has been set."

"Perhaps the death of Monsignor Gaetani will delay it."

"Why?"

"Because it will mean one more unpleasant experience for you."

"I'm not selfish. I realize that my daughter will be happy in the convent, much happier than here with me, and I've resigned myself to it."

"Does María Rosario's calling go far back?"

"To her childhood."

"And she hasn't fluctuated?"

"Never!"

I smoothed my mustache with a somewhat shaky hand:

"Her calling is like a saint's."

"Yes, a saint's . . . I'd have you know that it isn't the first in our family. Saint Margarita of Ligura, abbess of Fiesole, was the daughter of a Prince Gaetani. Her remains are preserved in the palace chapel, and after four hundred years she looks as if she had just died: she seems to be sleeping. You haven't been down to the crypt?"

"No, madam."

"Well, you must go down some day."

We remained silent. The princess began sighing again, her hands raised to her forehead. Her daughters, at the far end of the room, were conversing in low tones. I looked at them with a smile and they responded in the same way, with a certain childlike, mocking jollity that contrasted with their black mourning dresses. The afternoon was beginning to fade away, and the princess had her servants open a window that overlooked the garden:

"Girls, the scent of those roses is making me sick!"

And she pointed to the vases on her vanity table. When the window was open, a light breeze entered the room. It was merry, fragrant, and pleasant as a message from springtime. Its invisible wings stirred the

taron los rizos de aquellas cabezas juveniles, que allá en el fondo de la estancia me miraban y me sonreían. ¡Rizos rubios, dorados, luminosos, cabezas adorables, cuántas veces os he visto en mis sueños pecadores más bellas que esas aladas cabezas angélicas que solían ver en sus sueños celestiales los santos ermitaños!

La Princesa se acostó al comienzo de la noche, poco después del rosario. En el salón medio apagado, hablaban en voz baja las viejas damas que desde hacía veinte años acudían regularmente a la tertulia del Palacio Gaetani: Comenzaba a sentirse el calor, y estaban abiertas las puertas de cristales que daban al jardín. Dos hijas de la Princesa, María Soledad y María del Carmen hacían los honores: La conversación era lánguida, de una languidez apocada y beata. Afortunadamente, al sonar las nueve en el reloj de la Catedral, las señoras se levantaron, y María del Carmen y María Soledad salieron acompañándolas. Yo quedé solo en el vasto salón, y no sabiendo qué hacer, bajé al jardín.

Era una noche de Primavera, silenciosa y fragante. El aire agitaba las ramas de los árboles con blando movimiento, y la luna iluminaba por un instante la sombra y el misterio de los follajes. Sentíase pasar por el jardín un largo estremecimiento y luego todo quedaba en esa amorosa paz de las noches serenas. En el azul profundo temblaban las estrellas, y la quietud del jardín parecía mayor que la quietud del cielo. A lo lejos, el mar misterioso y ondulante exhalaba su eterna queja. Las dormidas olas fosforescían al pasar tumbando los delfines, y una vela latina cruzaba el horizonte bajo la luna pálida.

Yo recorría un sendero orillado por floridos rosales: Las luciérnagas brillaban al pie de los arbustos, el aire era fragante, y el más leve soplo bastaba para deshojar en los tallos las rosas marchitas. Yo sentía esa vaga y romántica tristeza que encanta los enamoramientos juveniles, con la leyenda de los grandes y trágicos dolores que se visten a la usanza antigua. Consideraba la herida de mi corazón como aquellas que no tienen cura y pensaba que de un modo fatal decidiría mi suerte. Con extremos verterianos soñaba superar a todos los amantes que en el mundo han sido, y por infortunados y leales pasaron a la historia, y aun asomaron más de una vez la faz lacrimosa en las cantigas del vulgo. Desgraciadamente, quedéme sin superarlos, porque tales romanticismos nunca fueron otra cosa que un perfume derramado sobre todos mis amores de juventud. ¡Locuras gentiles y fugaces que

curls on the youthful heads of the girls looking at me and smiling to me from the far end of the room. Blonde, golden, luminous curls, lovable heads, how often I have seen you in my sinful dreams looking more lovely than those winged angelic heads which holy hermits used to see in their heavenly dreams!

The princess went to bed at nightfall, shortly after saying the rosary. In the semidarkness of the salon, the old ladies who had regularly attended the Gaetani palace conversation circle for twenty years were conversing in low tones. The heat was beginning to be noticeable, and the glass-paned doors leading to the garden were open. Two of the princess's daughters, María Soledad and María del Carmen, were presiding. The conversation was languid, in a timid and devout way. Fortunately, when the cathedral clock struck nine, the ladies rose, and María del Carmen and María Soledad went out to accompany them. I was left alone in the vast salon and, not knowing what to do, I went down into the garden.

It was a spring night, quiet and fragrant. The breeze was stirring the branches of the trees with a gentle motion, and the moon for an instant was illuminating the shade and the mystery of the foliage. A long shudder could be felt passing through the garden, and then everything remained in that amorous peace of serene nights. In the deep blue the stars were twinkling, and the quietude of the garden seemed greater than that of the sky. In the distance, the mysterious, rippling sea was breathing its eternal plaint. The dormant waves had a phosphorescent glow when the dolphins plunged by, and a lateen sail crossed the horizon beneath the pallid moon.

I was following a path lined by blossoming rosebushes. The fireflies were gleaming at the foot of the shrubbery, the air was fragrant, and the slightest puff was sufficient to blow the petals off the withered roses on their stems. I felt that vague, romantic sadness which enchants youthful infatuations with the legend of the great, tragic sorrows that wear the garb of yesteryear. I considered my heart's wound to be one of the incurable kind, and I thought that it would determine my destiny in a fateful way. With Werther-like excess, I dreamed of surpassing all the lovers who have ever lived, who have become the stuff of history for their ill fortune and faithfulness, and who have even frequently shown their tearstained faces in folk songs. Unfortunately, I have never been able to surpass them, because such romantic notions have never been more than a scent sprinkled over all

duraban algunas horas, y que, sin duda por eso, me han hecho suspirar y sonreír toda la vida!

De pronto huyeron mis pensamientos. Daba las doce el viejo reloj de la Catedral y cada campanada, en el silencio del jardín, retumbó con majestad sonora. Volví al salón, donde ya estaban apagadas las luces. En los cristales de una ventana temblaba el reflejo de la luna, y allá en el fondo, brillaba la esfera de un reloj que con delicado y argentino son, daba también las doce. Me detuve en la puerta, para acostumbrarme a la oscuridad, y poco a poco mis ojos columbraron la forma incierta de las cosas. Una mujer hallábase sentada en el sofá del estrado. Yo sólo distinguía sus manos blancas: El cuerpo era una sombra negra. Quise acercarme, y vi cómo sin ruido se ponía en pie y cómo sin ruido se alejaba y desaparecía. Hubiérala creído un fantasma engaño de mis ojos, si al dejar de verla no llegase hasta mí un sollozo. Al pie del sofá estaba caído un pañuelo perfumado de rosas y húmedo de llanto. Lo besé con afán. No dudaba que aquel fantasma había sido María Rosario.

Pasé la noche en vela, sin conseguir conciliar el sueño. Vi rayar el alba en las ventanas de mi alcoba, y sólo entonces, en medio del alegre voltear de un esquilón que tocaba a misa, me dormí. Al despertarme, ya muy entrado el día, supe con profundo reconocimiento cuánto por la salud de mi alma se interesaba la Princesa Gaetani. La noble señora estaba muy afligida porque yo había perdido el Oficio Divino.

Al caer de la tarde llegaron aquellas dos señoras de los cabellos blancos y los negros y crujientes vestidos de seda. La Princesa se incorporó saludándolas con amable y desfallecida voz:

—¿Dónde habéis estado?

—¡Hemos corrido toda Ligura!

—¡Vosotras!

Ante el asombro de la Princesa, las dos señoras se miraron sonriendo:

—Cuéntale tú, Antonina.

—Cuéntale tú, Lorencina.

Y luego las dos comienzan el relato al mismo tiempo: Habían oído un sermón en la Catedral: Habían pasado por el Convento de las Carmelitas para preguntar por la Madre Superiora que estaba enferma: Habían velado al Santísimo. Aquí la Princesa interrumpió:

my youthful amours. Pleasant, fleeting follies that lasted a few hours and, no doubt for that very reason, have made me sigh and smile all my life!

Suddenly my thoughts fled. The old cathedral clock was striking twelve and, in the silence of the garden, every tone reechoed with sonorous majesty. I returned to the salon, where the lights had already been put out. The reflection of the moon was trembling on the panes of a window, and at the far end there gleamed the round face of a clock that was also striking twelve with a delicate, silvery sound. I halted in the doorway to get used to the darkness, and gradually my eyes made out the vague form of the objects in the room. A woman was sitting on the drawing-room sofa. All I could distinguish was her white hands. Her body was a black shadow. I wanted to approach, and I saw her stand up noiselessly and move away and vanish noiselessly. I would have thought her an optical illusion if, just as she disappeared, a sob hadn't reached me. At the foot of the sofa had fallen a handkerchief scented with roses and damp with tears. I kissed it with anxiety. I had no doubt that that specter was María Rosario.

I spent the night awake, unable to fall asleep. I saw the dawn shine into my bedroom windows, and only then, amid the merry pealing of a bell ringing for mass, did I doze off. When I awoke, already well into the day, I learned with deep gratitude just how concerned Princess Gaetani was for the welfare of my soul. That noble lady was quite distressed because I had missed the divine service.

When evening fell, those two ladies with white hair and rustling black silk dresses arrived. The princess sat up, greeting them in a friendly but faint voice:

"Where have you been?"

"We've run all over Ligura!"

"You?!"

At the princess's amazement the two ladies looked at each other with a smile:

"You tell her, Antonina!"

"You tell her, Lorenzina!"

And then they both began their narrative at the same time. They had listened to a sermon in the cathedral. They had stopped by the Carmelite convent to inquire after the Mother Superior, who was ill. They had assisted in the communion service. At that point the princess interrupted them:

—¿Y cómo sigue la Madre Superiora?

—Todavía no baja al locutorio.

—¿A quién habéis visto?

—A la Madre Escolástica. ¡La pobre siempre tan buena y tan cariñosa! No sabes cuánto nos preguntó por ti y por tus hijas: Nos enseñó el hábito de María Rosario: Iba a mandárselo para que lo probase: Lo ha cosido ella misma: Dice que será el último, porque está casi ciega.

La Princesa suspiró:

—¡Yo no sabía que estuviese ciega!

—Ciega no, pero ve muy poco.

—Pues no tiene años para eso . . .

La Princesa acabó la frase con un gesto de fatiga, llevándose las manos a la frente. Después se distrajo mirando hacia la puerta, donde asomaba la escuálida figura del Señor Polonio. Detenido en el umbral, el mayordomo saludaba con una profunda reverencia:

—¿Da su permiso mi Señora la Princesa?

—Adelante, Polonio. ¿Qué ocurre?

—Ha venido el sacristán de las Madres Carmelitas con el hábito de la Señorina.

—¿Y ella lo sabe?

—Probándoselo queda.

Al oír esto, las otras hijas de la Princesa, que sentadas en rueda bordaban el manto de Santa Margarita de Ligura, habláronse en voz baja, juntando las cabezas, y salieron de la estancia con alegre murmullo, en un grupo casto y primaveral como aquel que pintó Sandro Boticelli. La Princesa las miró con maternal orgullo, y luego hizo un ademán despidiendo al mayordomo, que, en lugar de irse, adelantó algunos pasos balbuciendo:

—Ya he dado el último perfil al Paso de las Caídas . . . Hoy empiezan las procesiones de Semana Santa.

La Princesa replicó con desdeñosa altivez:

—Y sin duda has creído que yo lo ignoraba.

El mayordomo pareció consternado:

—¡Líbreme el Cielo, Señora!

—¿Pues entonces . . . ?

—Hablando de las procesiones, el sacristán de las Madres me dijo que tal vez este año no saliesen las que costea y patrocina mi Señora la Princesa.

—¿Y por qué causa?

—Por la muerte de Monseñor, y el luto de la casa.

"And how is the Mother Superior getting on?"

"She still isn't coming down to the visiting room."

"Whom did you see?"

"The mother who teaches theology. The poor woman, always so good and affectionate! You don't know how much she asked us about you and your daughters. She showed us María Rosario's habit. She was going to send it to her to try it on. She sewed it herself. She says it will be the last one, because she's nearly blind."

The princess sighed:

"I didn't know she was blind!"

"Not blind, but her sight is very bad."

"But she isn't old enough for that . . ."

The princess terminated her sentence with a gesture of fatigue, raising her hands to her forehead. Then she was distracted, looking toward the doorway, where the scrawny figure of Master Polonio appeared. Stationary on the threshold, the butler greeted her with a low bow:

"Do I have the princess's permission?"

"Come in, Polonio. What's happening?"

"The sacristan of the Carmelite Mothers has arrived with the signorina's habit"

"Does she know?"

"She's trying it on right now."

When they heard this, the princess's other daughters, who were sitting in a ring embroidering the mantle of Saint Margarita of Ligura, conversed in low tones, putting their heads together, and left the room murmuring merrily, in a chaste, vernal group like that painted by Sandro Botticelli. The princess looked at them with motherly pride, and then made a gesture of dismissal to the butler, who, instead of going, walked a few steps forward, stammering:

"I've already put the finishing touches on the tableau of the Way of the Cross . . . The Holy Week processions are beginning today."

The princess retorted with scornful haughtiness:

"And no doubt you thought I didn't know."

The butler seemed to be dismayed:

"God forbid, madam!"

"Well, then? . . ."

"Speaking of the processions, the sacristan of the Carmelites told me that perhaps this year the ones that you subsidize and sponsor won't take place, princess."

"And for what reason?"

"Because of the Monsignor's death, and the house being in mourning."

—Nada tiene que ver con la religión, Polonio.

Aquí la Princesa creyó del caso suspirar. El mayordomo se inclinó:

—Cierto, Señora, ciertísimo. El sacristán lo decía contemplando mi obra. Ya sabe la Señora Princesa . . . El Paso de las Caídas . . . Espero que mi Señora se digne verlo . . .

El mayordomo se detuvo sonriendo ceremoniosamente. La Princesa asintió con un gesto, y luego volviéndose a mí pronunció con ligera ironía:

—¿Tú acaso ignoras que mi mayordomo es un gran artista?

El viejo se inclinó:

—¡Un artista . . . ! Hoy día ya no hay artistas. Los hubo en la antigüedad.

Yo intervine con mi juvenil insolencia:

—¿Pero de qué época sois, Señor Polonio?

El mayordomo repuso sonriendo:

—Vos tenéis razón, Excelencia . . . Hablando con verdad, no puedo decir que éste sea mi siglo . . .

—Vos pertenecéis a la antigüedad más clásica y más remota. ¿Y cuál arte cultiváis, Señor Polonio?

El Señor Polonio repuso con suma modestia:

—Todas, Excelencia.

—¡Sois un nieto de Miguel Ángel!

—El cultivarlas todas no quiere decir que sea maestro en ellas, Excelencia.

La Princesa sonrió con aquella amable ironía que al mismo tiempo mostraba señoril y compasivo afecto por el viejo mayordomo:

—Xavier, tienes que ver su última obra: ¡El Paso de las Caídas! ¡Una maravilla!

Las dos ancianas juntaron las secas manos con infantil admiración:

—¡Si cuando joven hubiera querido ir a Roma . . . ! ¡Oh!

El mayordomo lloraba enternecido:

—¡Señoras . . . ! ¡Mis nobles Mecenas!

De pronto se oyó murmullo de juveniles voces que se aproximaban, y un momento después el coro de las cinco hermanas invadía la estancia. María Rosario traía puesto el blanco hábito que debía llevar durante toda la vida, y las otras se agrupaban en torno como si fuese una Santa. Al verlas entrar, la Princesa se incorporó muy pálida: Las lágrimas acudían a sus ojos y luchaba en vano por retenerlas. Cuando María Rosario se acercó a besarle la mano, le echó los brazos al cuello y la estrechó amorosamente. Quedó después, contemplándola, y no pudo contener un grito de angustia.

❊   ❊   ❊

"That has nothing to do with religious duties, Polonio."

At that point the princess thought it fitting to sigh. The butler bowed:

"True, madam, most true. The sacristan said as much while he was looking at my work. As the princess surely knows . . . the tableau of the Way of the Cross . . . I hope my lady will deign to view it . . ."

The butler stopped, and smiled ceremoniously. The princess consented with a gesture, and then, turning to me, she said with a touch of irony:

"Perhaps you're unaware that my butler is a great artist?"

The old man bowed:

"Artist! . . . There are no artists today. There used to be long, long ago."

I intervened with my youthful insolence:

"But what era do you belong to, Master Polonio?"

The butler replied with a smile:

"You're right, Excellency . . . Speaking honestly, I can't say that this is my century . . ."

"You belong to more classical and more remote antiquity. And what art do you practice, Master Polonio?"

Master Polonio replied with extreme modesty:

"All of them, Excellency."

"You're a descendant of Michelangelo!"

"Practicing them all isn't the same as being a master of them, Excellency."

The princess smiled with that amiable irony which was obviously at the same time an aristocratic, sympathetic affection for her old butler.

"Xavier, you must see his latest creation. The tableau of the Way of the Cross! A marvel!"

The two old ladies clasped their withered hands in childlike admiration:

"Imagine: when he was young he wanted to go to Rome . . . ! Oh!"

The butler was weeping with emotion:

"Ladies . . . ! My noble patrons!"

All at once was heard a murmur of youthful voices coming closer, and a moment later the chorus of five sisters invaded the room. María Rosario had put on the white habit that she was to wear for the rest of her life, and the others formed a group around her as if she were a saint. On seeing them enter, the princess sat up, very pale. Tears welled up in her eyes as she fought in vain to repress them. When María Rosario came up to kiss her hand, she threw her arms around her neck and hugged her lovingly. Then she kept observing her, unable to suppress a cry of anguish.

❖   ❖   ❖

Yo estaba tan conmovido que, como en sueños, percibí la voz del viejo mayordomo: Hablaba después de un profundo silencio:

—Si merezco el honor . . . Perdonad, pero ahora van a llevarse esa pobre obra de mis manos pecadoras. Si queréis verla, apenas queda tiempo . . .

Las dos señoras se levantaron sacudiéndose las crujientes y arrugadas faldas:

—¡Oh . . . ! Vamos allá.

Antes de salir ya comenzaron las explicaciones del Señor Polonio:

—Conviene saber que el Nazareno y el Cirineo son los mismos que había antiguamente. De mi mano son únicamente los judíos. Los hice de cartón. Ya conocen mi antigua manía de hacer caretas. Una manía y de las peores. Con ella di gran impulso a los Carnavales, que es la fiesta de Satanás. ¡Aquí antes nadie se vestía de máscara, pero como yo regalaba a todo el mundo mis caretas de cartón! ¡Dios me perdone! Los Carnavales de Ligura llegaron a ser famosos en Italia . . . Vengan por aquí sus Excelencias.

Pasamos a una gran sala que tenía las ventanas cerradas. El Señor Polonio adelantóse para abrirlas. Después se volvió pidiendo mil perdones, y nosotros entramos. Mis ojos quedaron extasiados al ver en medio de la sala unas andas con Jesús Nazareno, entre cuatro judíos torvos y barbudos. Las dos señoras lloraban de emoción:

—¡Si considerásemos lo que Nuestro Señor padeció por nosotros!

—¡Ay . . . ! ¡Si lo considerásemos!

En presencia de aquellos cuatro judíos vestidos a la chamberga, era indudable que las devotas señoras procuraban hacerse cargo del drama de la Pasión. El Señor Polonio daba vueltas en torno de las andas, y con los nudillos golpeaba suavemente las fieras cabezas de los cuatro deicidas:

—¡De cartón . . . ! ¡Sí, señoras, igual que las caretas! Fue una idea que me vino sin saber cómo.

Las damas repetían juntando las manos:

—¡Inspiración divina . . . !

—¡Inspiración de lo alto . . . !

El Señor Polonio sonreía:

—Nadie, absolutamente nadie, esperaba que pudiese realizar la idea . . . Se burlaban de mí . . . Ahora, en cambio, todo se vuelven

I was so moved that I heard the old butler's voice as if in a dream. He was speaking after a deep silence:

"If I deserve the honor . . . Forgive me, but now this poor creation of my sinful hands is being taken away. If you wish to see it, there's hardly time . . ."

The two ladies rose, shaking out their rustling, wrinkled skirts:

"Oh . . . ! Let's go!"

Even before leaving, Master Polonio's explanations had begun:

"You ought to know that the figures of Jesus and Simon of Cyrene are the ones that were there before. Only the Jews are by my hand. I made them of cardboard. You're aware of my longtime craze for making masks. A craze, and one of the worst. With it I gave great momentum to the Carnival celebrations, which are Satan's holiday. Before then, no one here masqueraded, but since I gave my cardboard masks away to everyone . . . ! May God forgive me! The Ligura Carnivals got to be famous all over Italy . . . Come this way, Your Excellencies."

We proceeded to a large room where the windows were closed. Master Polonio walked ahead to open them. Then he turned back to us, asking a thousand pardons, and we went in. My eyes were enraptured to see in the center of the room a carrying platform with Jesus of Nazareth amid four grim, bearded Jews. The two ladies were weeping with emotion:

"If we only pondered on how much Our Lord suffered for our sake!"

"Ah . . . ! If we only pondered on it!"

In the presence of those four Jews dressed in long coats,[9] there was no doubt that the pious ladies were trying to take upon themselves the drama of the Passion. Master Polonio was walking round and round the platform, gently tapping with his knuckles the fierce heads of the four deicides:

"Of cardboard . . . ! Yes, ladies, just like the masks! I don't know how I got the idea."

Clasping their hands, the ladies kept repeating:

"A divine inspiration . . . !"

"An inspiration from on high . . . !"

Master Polonio was smiling:

"Nobody, absolutely nobody thought I was able to execute the idea . . . They were making fun of me . . . But now everyone is congratu-

9. The Spanish expression *a la chamberga* commemorates a uniform introduced by Friedrich Hermann von Schönberg (1615–1690), a German who served Louis XIV (as the Comte de Schomberg), rising to the rank of marshal.

parabienes. ¡Y yo perdono aquellos sarcasmos! ¡Llevé mi idea en la frente un año entero!

Oyéndole, las señoras, repetían enternecidas:

—¡Inspiración . . . !

—¡Inspiración . . . !

Jesús Nazareno, desmelenado, lívido, sangriento, agobiado bajo el peso de la cruz, parecía clavar en nosotros su mirada dulce y moribunda. Los cuatro judíos, vestidos de rojo, le rodeaban fieros. El que iba delante tocaba la trompeta. Los que le daban escolta a uno y otro lado, llevaban sendas disciplinas, y aquel que caminaba detrás, mostraba al pueblo la sentencia de Pilatos. Era un papel de música, y el mayordomo tuvo cuidado de advertirnos cómo en aquel tiempo de gentiles, los escribanos hacían unos garabatos muy semejantes a los que hacen los músicos. Volviéndose a mí con gravedad doctoral, continuó:

—Los moros y los judíos todavía escriben de una manera semejante. ¿Verdad, Excelencia?

Cuando el Señor Polonio se hallaba en esta erudita explicación, llegó un sacristán capitaneando a cuatro devotos que venían para llevarse a la iglesia de los Capuchinos aquel famoso Paso de las Caídas. El Señor Polonio cubrió las andas con una colcha, y les ayudó a levantarlas. Después los acompañó hasta la puerta de la estancia:

—¡Cuidado . . . ! No tropezar con las paredes . . . ! ¡Cuidado . . . !

Enjugóse las lágrimas, y abrió una ventana para verlos salir. La primera preocupación del sacristán, cuando asomó en la calle, fue mirar al cielo, que estaba completamente encapotado. Luego se puso al frente de su tropa, y echó por medio. Los cuatro devotos iban casi corriendo. Las andas envueltas en la colcha roja bamboleaban sobre sus hombros. El Señor Polonio se dirigió a nosotros:

—Sin cumplimiento: ¿Qué les ha parecido?

Las dos señoras estuvieron, como siempre, de acuerdo:

—¡Edificante!

—¡Edificante!

El Señor Polonio sonrió beatíficamente y su escuálida figura de dómine enamorado de las musas, se volvió a la ventana con la mano extendida hacia la calle, para enterarse si llovía.

Aquella noche las hijas de la Princesa habíanse refugiado en la te-

lating me. And I forgive those sarcasms! I had the idea in my head for a whole year!"

Hearing him, the ladies repeated with emotion:

"Inspiration . . . !"

"Inspiration . . . !"

Jesus of Nazareth, disheveled, livid, bloodied, bowed down beneath the weight of the cross, seemed to be fixing on us his gentle, dying gaze. The four Jews, dressed in red, encircled him fiercely. The one who walked in front was blowing a trumpet. Those who escorted him on either side carried scourges, and the one who walked behind was displaying to the spectators the sentence delivered by Pilate. It was a sheet of music paper, and the butler took care to inform us that in those heathen days scribes made scrawls very similar to those which musicians make. Addressing me with professorial gravity, he went on:

"The Moors and the Jews still write in a similar way. Isn't that so, Excellency?"

While Master Polonio was engaged in this erudite explanation, a sacristan arrived, in charge of four devotees who had come to carry that famous tableau of the Way of the Cross to the church of the Capuchins. Master Polonio covered the platform with a counterpane, and helped them lift it. Then he accompanied them to the door of the room:

"Careful . . . ! Don't bump into the walls . . . Careful . . . !"

He wiped away his tears, and opened a window to watch them leave.[10] The sacristan's first concern, on reaching the street, was to look at the sky, which was totally overcast. Then he took the lead of his troop, and dashed ahead recklessly. The four devotees were nearly running. The platform, wrapped in the red counterpane, was wobbling on their shoulders. Master Polonio addressed us:

"All compliments aside: what did you think of it?"

The two ladies were in agreement, as always:

"Edifying!"

"Edifying!"

Master Polonio smiled beatifically, and his skinny figure, that of a pedant in love with the Muses, turned to the window, his hand outheld toward the street, to see if it was raining.

That night, the princess's daughters had taken refuge on the ter-

---

10. Perhaps he hadn't opened *all* the window shutters previously.

rraza, bajo la luna, como las hadas de los cuentos: Rodeaban a una amiga joven y muy bella, que de tiempo en tiempo me miraba llena de curiosidad. En el salón, las señoras ancianas conversaban discretamente, y sonreían al oír las voces juveniles que llegaban en ráfagas perfumadas con el perfume de las lilas que se abrían al pie de la terraza. Desde el salón distinguíase el jardín, inmóvil bajo la luna, que envolvía en pálida claridad la cima mustia de los cipreses y el balconaje de la terraza donde, otras veces, el pavo real abría su abanico de quimera y de cuento.

Yo quise varias veces acercarme a María Rosario. Todo fue inútil: Ella adivinaba mis intenciones, y alejábase cautelosa, sin ruido, con la vista baja y las manos cruzadas sobre el escapulario del hábito monjil que conservaba puesto. Viéndola a tal extremo temerosa, yo sentía halagado mi orgullo donjuanesco, y algunas veces, sólo por turbarla, cruzaba de un lado al otro. La pobre niña al instante se prevenía para huir: Yo pasaba aparentando no advertirlo. Tenía la petulancia de los veinte años. Otros momentos entraba en el salón y deteníame al lado de las viejas damas, que recibían mis homenajes con timidez de doncellas. Recuerdo que me hallaba hablando con aquella devota Marquesa de Téscara, cuando, movido por un oscuro presentimiento, volví la cabeza y busqué con los ojos la blanca figura de María Rosario. La Santa ya no estaba.

Una nube de tristeza cubrió mi alma. Dejé a la vieja linajuda y salí a la terraza. Mucho tiempo permanecí reclinado sobre el florido balconaje de piedra contemplando el jardín. En el silencio perfumado cantaba un ruiseñor, y parecía acordar su voz con la voz de las fuentes. El reflejo de la luna iluminaba aquel sendero de los rosales que yo había recorrido otra noche. El aire suave y gentil, un aire a propósito para llevar suspiros, pasaba murmurando, y a lo lejos, entre mirtos inmóviles, ondulaba el agua de un estanque. Yo evocaba en la memoria el rostro de María Rosario, y no cesaba de pensar:

—¿Qué siente ella . . . ? ¿Qué siente ella por mí . . . ?

Bajé lentamente hacia el estanque. Las ranas que estaban en la orilla saltaron al agua produciendo un ligero estremecimiento en el dormido cristal. Había allí un banco de piedra y me senté. La noche y la luna eran propicias al ensueño, y pude sumergirme en una contemplación semejante al éxtasis. Confusos recuerdos de otros tiempos y otros amores se levantaron en mi memoria. Todo el pasado resurgía como una gran tristeza y un gran remordimiento. Mi juventud me parecía mar de soledad y de tormentas, siempre en noche. El alma

race, beneath the moon, like the fairies in folktales. They encircled a young, very beautiful girlfriend, who looked at me with great curiosity every so often. In the salon, the old ladies were chatting discreetly, smiling when they heard the youthful voices borne on gusts perfumed with the perfume of the lilacs that were opening at the foot of the terrace. From the salon the garden could be clearly seen, motionless beneath the moon, which was enveloping in pale light the parched tops of the cypresses and the terrace balcony, where at times the peacock spread out its chimerical, fairy-tale fan.

Several times I tried to approach María Rosario. Each time in vain: she guessed my intentions and moved away cautiously, soundlessly, her eyes downcast and her hands crossed over the scapulary of the nun's habit she was still wearing. Seeing her timorous to that extent, I felt flattered in my Don Juan's pride, and a few times, merely to upset her, I walked from one side to another. Instantly the poor girl would make ready to flee. I would pass by, pretending not to notice. I had a twenty-year-old's arrogance. At other times I'd enter the salon and linger beside the old ladies, who received my homage with maidenly shyness. I recall that I was engaged in speaking with that devout Marquise of Téscara when, prompted by some obscure foreboding, I turned my head and looked for María Rosario's white form. The saint was no longer there.

A cloud of sadness covered my soul. I abandoned the highborn old lady and went out onto the terrace. I remained for quite some time leaning over the florid stone balcony and observing the garden. In the fragrant silence a nightingale was singing, and it seemed to attune its voice to the voice of the fountains. The reflection of the moon was illuminating that rosebush-lined path which I had walked down that other night. The soft, gentle breeze, a breeze just made for carrying sighs, passed by with a murmur, and in the distance, between motionless myrtles, the water of a pool was rippling. I evoked in my memory the face of María Rosario, and I thought endlessly:

"What does she feel? . . . What does she feel for me? . . ."

I slowly descended to the pool. The frogs on its banks hopped into the water, causing a slight shudder on its dormant glassy surface. A stone bench was located there, and I sat down. The night and the moonlight were favorable to reverie, and I found myself sunk in a contemplation similar to ecstasy. Confused recollections of other days and other romances loomed up in my memory. The whole past rose anew like a great sadness and a great remorse. My youth seemed to me like a sea of solitude and storm, in perpetual night. My soul was languish-

languidecía en el recogimiento del jardín, y el mismo pensamiento
volvía como el motivo de un canto lejano:

—¿Qué siente ella . . . ? ¿Qué siente ella por mí . . . ?

Ligeras nubes blancas erraban en torno de la luna y la seguían en
su curso fantástico y vagabundo. Empujadas por un soplo invisible, la
cubrieron y quedó sumido en sombras el jardín. El estanque dejó de
brillar entre los mirtos inmóviles: Sólo la cima de los cipreses permaneció iluminada. Como para armonizar con la sombra, se levantó
una brisa que pasó despertando largo susurro en todo el recinto y
trajo hasta mí el aroma de las rosas deshojadas. Lentamente volví
hacia el Palacio: Mis ojos se detuvieron en una ventana iluminada, y
no sé qué oscuro presentimiento hizo palpitar mi corazón. Aquella
ventana alzábase apenas sobre la terraza, permanecía abierta, y el
aire ondulaba la cortina. Me pareció que por el fondo de la estancia
cruzaba una sombra blanca. Quise acercarme, pero el rumor de unas
pisadas bajo la avenida de los cipreses me detuvo. El viejo major-
domo paseaba a la luz de la luna sus ensueños de artista. Yo quedé inmóvil en el fondo del jardín. Y contemplando aquella luz el corazón
latía:

—¿Qué siente ella . . . ? ¿Qué siente ella por mí . . . ?

¡Pobre María Rosario! Yo la creía enamorada, y, sin embargo, mi
corazón presentía no sé qué quimérica y confusa desventura. Quise
volver a sumergirme en mi amoroso ensueño, pero el canto de un sapo
repetido monótonamente bajo la arcada de los cipreses distraía y
turbaba mi pensamiento. Recuerdo que de niño he leído muchas
veces en un libro de devociones donde rezaba mi abuela, que el
Diablo solía tomar ese aspecto para turbar la oración de un santo
monje. Era natural que a mí me ocurriese lo mismo. Yo, calumniado
y mal comprendido, nunca fui otra cosa que un místico galante, como
San Juan de la Cruz. En lo más florido de mis años hubiera dado gustoso todas las glorias mundanas para poder escribir en mis tarjetas: El
Marqués de Bradomín, Confesor de Princesas.

En achaques de amor, ¿quién no ha pecado alguna vez? Yo estoy ín-
timamente convencido de que el Diablo tienta siempre a los mejores.
Aquella noche el cornudo monarca del abismo encendió mi sangre con
su aliento de llamas y despertó mi carne flaca, fustigándola con su rabo
negro. Yo cruzaba la terraza cuando una ráfaga violenta alzó la
flameante cortina, y mis ojos mortales vieron arrodillada en el fondo de
la estancia la sombra pálida de María Rosario. No puedo decir lo que

ing in the seclusion of the garden, and the same thought returned over and over like the motif of a remote song:

"What does she feel? . . . What does she feel for me? . . ."

Light, white clouds were straying around the moon, following it in its fantastic, vagabond course. Impelled by an invisible breath, they covered it and the garden was plunged into darkness. The pool ceased gleaming between the motionless myrtles. Only the tops of the cypresses remained illuminated. As if to harmonize with the shadow, a breeze sprang up and passed by, arousing a lengthy whisper throughout the precincts and bringing me the fragrance of the petalless roses. Slowly I returned to the palace. My eyes remained fixed on a lighted window, and some obscure presentiment made my heart palpitate. That window was scarcely above the level of the terrace; it remained open, and the breeze was rippling the curtain. A white shadow seemed to be crossing the far end of the room. I wanted to approach, but the sound of footsteps under the avenue of the cypresses restrained me. The old butler was taking his artistic daydreams for a moonlight walk. I remained motionless at the back of the garden. And, as I viewed that light, my heart was beating:

"What does she feel? . . . What does she feel for me? . . ."

Poor María Rosario! I thought she was in love, and yet my heart foresaw some fanciful, unclear misfortune. I tried to reimmerse myself in my amorous reverie, but the croaking of a toad, monotonously repeated beneath the cypress arcade, distracted and muddled my thoughts. I recall that, as a boy, I frequently read in a prayer book which my grandmother used that the devil was wont to take on that shape to disturb the prayers of a holy monk. It was only natural that the same thing should be happening to me. Slandered and misunderstood, I have never been anything other than a gallant mystic, like Saint John of the Cross. In my most blossoming years I would gladly have given up all worldly glory to be able to write on my calling cards: "Marquis of Bradomín, confessor to princesses."

When sick with love, who has not sometimes sinned? I am firmly convinced that the devil always tempts the best among us. That night, the horned monarch of the abyss inflamed my blood with his fiery breath and aroused my weak flesh, lashing it with his black tail. I was crossing the terrace when a violent gust lifted the fluttering curtain and my mortal eyes beheld the pallid shadow of María Rosario kneeling at the far end of the room. I can't describe my sensations at that moment.

entonces pasó por mí. Creo que primero fue un impulso ardiente, y después una sacudida fría y cruel. La audacia que se admira en los labios y en los ojos de aquel retrato que del divino César Borgia pintó el divino Rafael de Sanzio. Me volví mirando en torno: Escuché un instante: En el jardín y en el Palacio todo era silencio. Llegué cauteloso a la ventana, y salté dentro. La Santa dio un grito: Se dobló blandamente como una flor cuando pasa el viento, y quedó tendida, desmayada, con el rostro pegado a la tierra. En mi memoria vive siempre el recuerdo de sus manos blancas y frías: ¡Manos diáfanas como la hostia . . . !

Al verla desmayada la cogí en brazos y la llevé a su lecho, que era como altar de lino albo y de rizado encaje. Después, con una sombra de recelo, apagué la luz: Quedó en tinieblas el aposento y con los brazos extendidos comencé a caminar en la oscuridad. Ya tocaba el borde de su lecho y percibía la blancura del hábito monjil, cuando el rumor de unos pasos en la terraza heló mi sangre y me detuvo. Manos invisibles alzaron la flameante cortina y la claridad de la luna penetró en la estancia. Los pasos habían cesado. Una sombra oscura se destacaba en el hueco iluminado de la ventana. La sombra se inclinó mirando hacia el fondo del aposento, y volvió a erguirse. Cayó la cortina, y escuché de nuevo el rumor de los pasos que se alejaban. Yo no había sido visto. Inmóvil, yerto, anhelante, permanecí sin moverme. De tiempo en tiempo la cortina temblaba: Un rayo de luna esclarecía el aposento, y con amoroso sobresalto mis ojos volvían a distinguir el cándido lecho y la figura cándida que yacía como la estatua en un sepulcro. Tuve miedo, y cauteloso llegué hasta la ventana. El sapo dejaba oír su canto bajo la arcada de los cipreses, y el jardín, húmedo y sombrío, susurrante y oscuro, parecía su reino. Salté la ventana como un ladrón, y anduve a lo largo de la terraza pegado al muro. De pronto, me pareció sentir leve rumor, como de alguno que camina recatándose. Me detuve y miré, pero en la inmensa sombra que el Palacio tendía sobre la terraza y el jardín, nada podía verse. Seguí adelante, y apenas había dado algunos pasos, cuando un aliento jadeante rozó mi cuello, y la punta de un puñal desgarró mi hombro. Me volví con fiera presteza. Un hombre corría a ocultarse en el jardín. Le reconocí con asombro, casi con miedo, al cruzar un claro iluminado por la luna, y desistí de seguirle, para evitar todo escándalo. Más, mucho más que la herida, me dolía dejar de castigarle, pero ello era forzoso, y entréme en el Palacio, sintiendo el calor tibio de la sangre correr por mi cuerpo. Musarelo, mi criado, que dormitaba en la antecámara, despertóse al ruido de mis pasos y encendió las luces de un candelabro. Después se cuadró militarmente:

I think that I first felt an ardent impulse, then a cold, cruel jolt. The boldness that one admires in the lips and eyes of that portrait of the divine Cesare Borgia painted by the divine Raffaello Sanzio! I turned and looked around. I listened for an instant. All was silence in the garden and the palace. Cautiously I went up to the window, and I leapt in. The saint uttered a cry. She doubled up gently, like a flower when the wind passes, and remained stretched out in a faint, her face glued to the floor. The recollection of her cold, white hands lives forever in my memory. Hands as translucent as the communion wafer . . . !

Seeing her in a swoon, I took her in my arms and carried her to her bed, which was like an altar of white linen and frilly lace. Then, with a touch of alarm, I put out the light. The room was plunged into shadow, and with outstretched arms I started to walk in the dark. I was touching the edge of her bed and sensing the whiteness of her nun's habit when the sound of footsteps on the terrace froze my blood and restrained me. Invisible hands lifted the fluttering curtain, and the brightness of the moonlight entered the room. The footsteps had ceased. A dark shadow was outlined in the illuminated recess of the window. The shadow stooped, looking toward the far end of the room, then straightened up again. The curtain fell, and again I heard the sound of the steps, now moving away. I had not been seen. Motionless, rigid, breathing hard, I didn't budge. Every so often the curtain trembled. A moonbeam lit up the room, and with an erotic start my eyes once again made out the white bed and the white figure lying there like a statue on a tomb. I was afraid, and I regained the window cautiously. The toad's croaking could be heard beneath the cypress arcade, and the garden, damp and somber, whispering and dark, seemed to be its kingdom. I leapt out the window like a burglar and walked the length of the terrace, hugging the wall. Suddenly I thought I heard a slight sound, as if someone were walking stealthily. I halted and looked around, but within the immense shadow that the palace cast on the terrace and the garden, nothing could be seen. I moved forward, but I had scarcely taken a few steps when a panting breath brushed my neck and the point of a dagger ripped my shoulder. I turned around with fierce promptness. A man was running to take cover in the garden. I recognized him in amazement, almost in fear, when he crossed a moonlit clearing, and I left off following him, to avoid a scandal. Much more painful than my wound was my failure to punish him, but it was unavoidable; and I entered the palace, feeling the warm blood running down my body. Musarello, my servant, who was dozing in the anteroom, awoke at the sound of my footsteps and lit the candles in a candelabrum. Then he stood at attention:

—A la orden, mi Capitán.

—Acércate, Musarelo . . .

Y tuve que apoyarme en la puerta para no caer. Musarelo era un soldado veterano que me servía desde mi entrada en la Guardia Noble. En voz baja y serena, le dije:

—Vengo herido . . .

Me miró con ojos asustados:

—¿Dónde, Señor?

—En el hombro.

Musarelo levantó los brazos, y clamó con la pasión religiosa de un fanático:

—¡A traición sería . . . !

Yo sonreí. Musarelo juzgaba imposible que un hombre pudiese herirme cara a cara:

—Sí, fue a traición. Ahora véndame, y que nadie se entere . . .

El soldado comenzó a desabrocharme la bizarra ropilla. Al descubrir la herida, yo sentí que sus manos temblaban:

—No te desmayes, Musarelo.

—No, mi Capitán.

Y todo el tiempo, mientras me curaba, estuvo repitiendo por lo bajo:

—¡Ya buscaremos a ese bergante . . . !

No, no era posible buscarle. El bergante estaba bajo la protección de la Princesa, y acaso en aquel instante le refería la hazaña de su puñal. Torturado por este pensamiento, pasé la noche inquieto y febril. Quería adivinar lo venidero, y perdíame en cavilaciones. Aún recuerdo que mi corazón tembló como el corazón de un niño, cuando volví a verme enfrente de la Princesa Gaetani.

Fue al entrar en la biblioteca, que por hallarse a oscuras yo había supuesto solitaria, cuando oí la voz apasionada de la Princesa Gaetani:

—¡Oh! ¡Cuánta infamia! ¡Cuánta infamia!

Desde aquel momento tuve por cierto que la noble señora lo sabía todo, y, cosa extraña, al dejar de dudar dejé de temer. Con la sonrisa en los labios y atusándome el mostacho entré en la biblioteca:

—Me pareció oíros, y no quise pasar sin saludaros, Princesa.

La Princesa estaba pálida como una muerta:

—¡Gracias!

"At your service, captain!"

"Come here, Musarello . . ."

And I had to lean against the door to keep from falling. Musarello was a veteran who had been my servant from the time I entered the noble guards. In low, calm tones I said:

"I've been wounded . . ."

He looked at me with frightened eyes:

"Where, sir?"

"On the shoulder."

Musarello raised his arms and exclaimed with the religious ardor of a fanatic:

"It must have been behind your back . . . !"

I smiled. Musarello deemed it impossible for a man to wound me face to face:

"Yes, it was behind my back. Now bandage me, and no one is to know . . ."

The soldier began to undo my elegant jacket. When he discovered the wound, I felt his hands trembling:

"Don't pass out, Musarello!"

"No, captain."

And all the time he was tending to me, he kept repeating quietly:

"We'll get that scoundrel . . . !"

No, it was impossible to get him. The scoundrel enjoyed the princess's protection, and perhaps at that very minute he was reporting the exploit of his dagger to her. Tormented by that thought, I spent the night restless and feverish. I wanted to guess what was to come, and I lost myself in musings. I still recall that my heart trembled like the heart of a child when I found myself once more in the presence of Princess Gaetani.

It was on entering the library, which I had supposed empty because it was in darkness, that I heard the impassioned voice of Princess Gaetani:

"Oh, how vile! How vile!"

From that moment on, I was sure that the noble lady knew everything. Strangely enough, as soon as my doubt was over my fear was over. With a smile on my lips, smoothing my mustache, I entered the library.

"I thought I heard you, and I didn't want to go by without greeting you, princess."

The princess was as pale as a dead woman:

"Thank you!"

En pie, tras el sillón que ocupaba la dama, hallábase el mayordomo, y en la penumbra de la biblioteca, yo le adivinaba asaetándome con los ojos. La Princesa inclinóse hojeando un libro. Sobre el vasto recinto se cernía el silencio como un murciélago de maleficio, que sólo se anuncia por el aire frío de sus alas. Yo comprendía que la noble señora buscaba herirme con su desdén, y un poco indeciso, me detuve en medio de la estancia. Mi orgullo levantábase en ráfagas, pero sobre los labios temblorosos estaba la sonrisa. Supe dominar mi despecho y me acerqué galante y familiar:

—¿Estáis enferma, señora?

—No . . .

La Princesa continuaba hojeando el libro, y hubo otro largo silencio. Al cabo suspiró dolorida, incorporándose en su sillón.

—Vámonos, Polonio . . .

El mayordomo me dirigió una mirada oblicua que me recordó al viejo Bandelone, que hacía los papeles de traidor en la compañía de Ludovico Straza:

—A vuestras órdenes, Excelencia.

Y la Princesa, seguida del mayordomo, sin mirarme, atravesó el largo salón de la biblioteca. Yo sentí la afrenta, pero todavía supe dominarme, y le dije:

—Princesa, esperad que os cuente cómo esta noche me han herido . . .

Y mi voz, helada por un temblor nervioso, tenía cierta amabilidad felina que puso miedo en el corazón de la Princesa. Yo la vi palidecer y detenerse mirando al mayordomo: Después murmuró fríamente, casi sin mover los labios:

—¿Dices que te han herido?

Su mirada se clavó en la mía, y sentí el odio en aquellos ojos redondos y vibrantes como los ojos de las serpientes. Un momento creí que llamase a sus criados para que me arrojasen del Palacio, pero temió hacerme tal afrenta, y desdeñosa siguió hasta la puerta, donde se volvió lentamente:

—¡Ah . . . ! No tuve carta autorizando tu estancia en Ligura.

Yo repuse sonriendo, sin apartar mis ojos de los suyos:

—Será preciso volver a escribir.

—¿Quién?

—Quien escribió antes: María Rosario . . .

La Princesa no esperaba tanta osadía, y tembló. Mi leyenda juvenil,

Standing behind the armchair in which the lady sat was the butler, and in the semidarkness of the library I guessed that he was looking daggers at me. The princess bent over and leafed through a book. Silence closed in over the vast space like an ill-omened bat which makes its presence known solely by the chilly breeze of its wings. I understood that the noble lady was trying to wound me with her contempt, and, somewhat undecided, I remained standing in the center of the room. My pride was rising up in gusts, but a smile lingered on my quivering lips. I was able to curb my indignation, and I approached gallantly and familiarly:

"Are you ill, madam?"

"No . . ."

The princess went on leafing through the book, and there was another long silence. Finally she sighed painfully, sitting up in her armchair.

"Let's go, Polonio . . ."

The butler gave me a sidewise glance that reminded me of old Bandelone, who used to play the role of villains in Ludovico Strazza's troupe:[11]

"At your service, Excellency."

And the princess, followed by her butler, crossed the long library room without looking at me. I was conscious of the insult, but I was still able to control myself, and I said to her:

"Princess, wait until I tell you about how I was wounded last night . . ."

And my voice, chilled by a nervous twitch, possessed a certain feline amiability which struck fear into the princess's heart. I saw her turn pale and halt, while looking at her butler. Then she murmured coldly, almost without moving her lips:

"You say you've been wounded?"

Her gaze was fixed on mine, and I felt the hatred in those eyes, round and vibrant as the eyes of serpents. For one moment I thought she would call her servants to have them throw me out of the palace, but she was afraid to affront me so badly, and she contemptuously made her way to the door, where she turned slowly:

"Ah . . . ! I never received a letter authorizing your stay in Ligura."

I answered with a smile, without moving my eyes away from hers:

"It will be necessary to write again."

"For whom?"

"For the one who wrote the first time: María Rosario . . ."

The princess hadn't been expecting brazenness of that sort, and she

---

11. Apparently these names are fictitious.

apasionada y violenta, ponía en aquellas palabras un nimbo satánico.
Los ojos de la Princesa se llenaron de lágrimas, y como eran todavía
muy bellos, mi corazón de andante caballero tuvo un remordimiento.
Por fortuna las lágrimas de la Princesa no llegaron a rodar, sólo em-
pañaron el claro iris de su pupila. Tenía el corazón de una gran dama
y supo triunfar del miedo: Sus labios se plegaron por el hábito de la
sonrisa, sus ojos me miraron con amable indiferencia y su rostro cobró
una expresión calma, serena, tersa, como esas santas de aldea que
parecen mirar benévolamente a los fieles. Detenida en la puerta, me
preguntó:

—¿Y cómo te han herido?

—En el jardín, señora . . .

La Princesa, sin moverse del umbral, escuchó la historia que yo
quise contarle. Atendía sin mostrar sorpresa, sin desplegar los labios,
sin hacer un gesto. Por aquel camino del mutismo intentaba que-
brantar mi audacia, y como yo adivinaba su intención me complacía
hablando sin reposo para velar su silencio. Mis últimas palabras
fueron acompañadas de una profunda cortesía, pero ya no tuve valor
para besarle la mano:

—¡Adiós, Princesa . . . ! Avisadme si tenéis noticias de Roma.

Polonio, a hurto, hizo los cuernos con la mano. La Princesa guardó
silencio. Crucé la silenciosa biblioteca y salí. Después, meditando a
solas si debía abandonar el Palacio Gaetani, resolví quedarme. Quería
mostrar a la Princesa que cuando suelen otros desesperarse, yo sabía
sonreír, y que donde otros son humillados, yo era triunfador. ¡El
orgullo ha sido siempre mi mayor virtud!

Permanecí todo el día retirado en mi cámara. Hallábame cansado
como después de una larga jornada, sentía en los párpados una aridez
febril, y sentía los pensamientos enroscados y dormidos dentro de mí,
como reptiles. A veces se despertaban y corrían sueltos, silenciosos, in-
decisos: Ya no eran aquellos pensamientos, de orgullo y de conquista,
que volaban como águilas con las garras abiertas. Ahora mi voluntad
flaqueaba, sentíame vencido y sólo quería abandonar el Palacio.
Hallábame combatido por tales bascas, cuando entró Musarelo:

—Mi Capitán, un padre capuchino desea hablaros.

—Dile que estoy enfermo.

—Se lo he dicho, Excelencia.

—Dile que me he muerto.

—Se lo he dicho, Excelencia.

trembled. My youthful reputation for passion and violence gave those words a satanic aura. The princess's eyes filled with tears, and since they were still very beautiful, my knight-errant's heart felt a touch of remorse. Fortunately the princess's tears didn't fall, but merely clouded the bright irises of her eyes. She had the bravery of a great lady and was able to vanquish fear. Her lips formed a smile through force of habit, her eyes looked at me with amiable indifference, and her face regained a calm, serene, smooth expression, like those images of saints in village churches which seem to gaze benevolently at the congregants. Stopping at the door, she asked me:

"And how were you wounded?"

"In the garden, madam . . ."

The princess, without leaving the threshold, listened to the story I saw fit to tell her. She heard me without showing surprise, without straightening her lips, without making a gesture. By that display of taciturnity she hoped to rattle my boldness, and since I guessed her intentions, I was pleased to speak on and on uninterruptedly, to keep watch over her silence. My last words were accompanied by a low bow, but by this time I didn't have the courage to kiss her hand:

"Farewell, princess . . . ! Let me know if you hear news from Rome."

Polonio secretly made a "horns" sign with his index and little fingers. The princess kept silent. I crossed the silent library and went out. Then, alone, I considered whether I ought to leave the Gaetani palace, but I decided to stay. I wanted to show the princess that when other men might give up hope, I was able to smile, and that where other men are humiliated, I was triumphant. Pride has always been my chief virtue!

I remained secluded in my room all day. I felt weary, as if after a long journey; I felt a feverish dryness on my eyelids, and I felt my thoughts coiled up asleep in me like reptiles. At times they awoke and ran loose, silent, indecisive. They were no longer those thoughts of pride and conquest which used to fly like eagles with open talons. Now my will was buckling, I felt subdued, and all I wanted was to leave the palace. I was still assailed by that nausea when Musarello came in:

"Captain, a Capuchin father wishes to speak with you."

"Tell him I'm ill."

"I did, Excellency."

"Tell him I'm dead."

"I did, Excellency."

Miré a Musarelo que permanecía ante mí con un gesto impasible y bufonesco:

—¿Pues entonces qué pretende ese padre capuchino?

—Rezaros los responsos, Excelencia.

Iba a replicar, pero en aquel momento una mano levantó el majestuoso cortinaje de terciopelo carmesí:

—Perdonad que os moleste, joven caballero.

Un viejo de luenga barba, vestido con el sayal de los capuchinos, estaba en el umbral de la puerta. Su aspecto venerable me impuso respeto:

—Entrad, Reverendo Padre.

Y adelantándome le ofrecí un sillón. El capuchino rehusó sentarse, y sus barbas de plata se iluminaron con la sonrisa grave y humilde de los Santos. Volvió a repetir:

—Perdonad que os moleste . . .

Hizo una pausa, esperando a que saliese Musarelo, y después continuó:

—Joven caballero, poned atención en cuanto voy a deciros, y líbreos el Cielo de menospreciar mi aviso. ¡Acaso pudiera costaros la vida! Prometedme que después de haberme oído no querréis saber más, porque responderos me sería imposible. Vos comprenderéis que este silencio lo impone un deber de mi estado religioso, y todo cristiano ha de respetarlo. ¡Vos sois cristiano . . . !

Yo repuse inclinándome profundamente:

—Soy un gran pecador, Reverendo Padre.

El rostro del capuchino volvió a iluminarse con indulgente sonrisa:

—Todos lo somos, hijo mío.

Después, con las manos juntas y los ojos cerrados, permaneció un momento como meditando. En las hundidas cuencas, casi se transparentaba el globo de los ojos bajo el velo descarnado y amarillento de los párpados. Al cabo de algún tiempo continuó:

—Mi palabra y mi fe no pueden seros sospechosas, puesto que ningún interés vil me trae a vuestra presencia. Solamente me guía una poderosa inspiración, y no dudo que es vuestro Ángel quien se sirve de mí para salvaros la vida, no pudiendo comunicar con vos. Ahora decidme si estáis conmovido, y si puedo daros el consejo que guardo en mi corazón.

—¡No lo dudéis, Reverendo Padre! Vuestras palabras me han hecho sentir algo semejante al terror. Yo juro seguir vuestro consejo, si en su ejecución no hallo nada contra mi honor de caballero.

I looked at Musarello, who stood there before me with an impassive, clownish expression:

"Then, what does that Capuchin father expect to do?"

"To say the prayers for the dead over you, Excellency."

I was about to retort, but at that moment a hand raised the majestic drapery of crimson velvet:

"Forgive me for disturbing you, young chevalier."

An old man with a long beard, dressed in the sackcloth of the Capuchins, was standing on the threshold of the door. His venerable appearance inspired me with respect:

"Come in, reverend father."

And I stepped forward to offer him an armchair. The Capuchin refused to sit down, and his silvery beard was illumined by the grave, humble smile of the saints. He repeated:

"Forgive me for disturbing you . . ."

He paused, waiting for Musarello to leave, then continued:

"Young chevalier, pay attention to what I am about to tell you, and may heaven keep you from ignoring my warning! It might cost you your life! Promise me that after hearing me out you won't try to learn anything further, because it would be impossible for me to answer you. You will understand that this silence is imposed by the obligations of my religious status, and every Christian must respect it. You are a Christian . . . !"

I replied with a low bow:

"I am a great sinner, reverend father."

Once again the Capuchin's face lit up with an indulgent smile:

"We all are, my son."

Then, his hands clasped and his eyes closed, he tarried a moment as if in meditation. In their deep sockets the spheres of his eyes nearly showed through the fleshless, yellowish veil of their lids. After a while he went on:

"My word and my honesty can arouse no suspicion in you, seeing that no base interest leads me to your presence. My only guide is a powerful inspiration, and I have no doubt that it's your guardian angel acting through me to save your life, being unable to communicate with you directly. Now tell me whether you are moved, and whether I can give you the advice that I hold in my heart."

"Have no doubt, reverend father! Your words have made me feel something akin to terror. I swear I will follow your advice, if in doing so I find nothing contrary to my honor as a gentleman."

—Está bien, hijo mío. Espero que por un sentimiento de caridad, suceda lo que suceda, a nadie hablaréis de este pobre capuchino.

—Lo prometo por mi fe de cristiano, Reverendo Padre . . . Pero hablad, os lo ruego.

—Hoy, después de anochecido, salid por la cancela del jardín, y bajad rodeando la muralla. Encontraréis una casa terreña que tiene en el tejado un cráneo de buey: Llamad allí. Os abrirá una vieja, y le diréis que deseáis hablarle: Con esto sólo os hará entrar. Es probable que ni siquiera os pregunte quién sois, pero si lo hiciese, dad un nombre supuesto. Una vez en la casa, rogadle que os escuche, y exigidle secreto sobre lo que vais a confiarle. Es pobre, y debéis mostraros liberal con ella, porque así os servirá mejor. Veréis como inmediatamente cierra su puerta para que podáis hablar sin recelo. Vos, entonces, hacedle entender que estáis resuelto a recobrar el anillo y cuanto ha recibido con él. No olvidéis esto: El anillo y cuanto ha recibido con él. Amenazadla si se resiste, pero no hagáis ruido, ni la dejéis que pida socorro. Procurad persuadirla ofreciéndole doble dinero del que alguien le ha ofrecido por perderos. Estoy seguro que acabará haciendo aquello que le mandéis, y que todo os costará bien poco. Pero aun cuando así no fuese, vuestra vida debe seros más preciada que todo el oro del Perú. No me preguntéis más, porque más no puedo deciros . . . Ahora, antes de abandonaros, juradme que estáis dispuesto a seguir mi consejo.

—Sí, Reverendo Padre, seguiré la inspiración del Ángel que os trajo.

—¡Así sea!

El capuchino trazó en el aire una lenta bendición, y yo incliné la cabeza para recibirla. Cuando salió, confieso que no tuve ánimos de reír. Con estupor, casi con miedo, advertí que en mi mano faltaba un anillo que llevaba desde hacía muchos años, y solía usar como sello. No pude recordar dónde lo había perdido. Era un anillo antiguo: Tenía el escudo grabado en amatista, y había pertenecido a mi abuelo el Marqués de Bradomín.

Bajé al jardín donde volaban los vencejos en la sombra azul de la tarde. Las veredas de mirtos seculares, hondas y silenciosas, parecían caminos ideales que convidaban a la meditación y al olvido, entre frescos aromas que esparcían en el aire las yerbas humildes que

"Good, my son. I hope that, no matter what happens, from a feeling of charity you will speak to no one about this poor Capuchin."

"I promise on my faith as a Christian, reverend father . . . But speak, I beg you."

"Today, after nightfall, go out through the garden gate and walk down the road, going around the wall. You will come across an earth-colored[12] house with an ox's skull on its roof. Knock at its door. An old woman will open it, and you'll tell her you want to talk to her. That will be enough for her to let you in. Probably she won't even ask you who you are, but if she should, give her a false name. Once inside the house, ask her to hear you out, and order her to keep secret whatever you confide in her. She's poor, and you ought to be generous to her, because that way she'll serve you better. You'll see her lock her door at once so you can speak without fear. Then you must give her to understand that you're determined to retrieve your ring and everything else she received along with it. Don't forget this: the ring and everything she received with it! Threaten her if she resists, but don't make noise or allow her to call for help. Try to persuade her by offering her twice the amount of money that she has been offered to destroy you. I'm sure she'll finally do what you order her to, and that the whole thing will cost you very little. But even if that should not be the case, your life ought to be more precious to you than all the gold in Peru. Don't ask me more, because I can't tell you more . . . Now, before I leave you, swear to me that you are willing to follow my advice."

"Yes, reverend father, I shall follow the inspiration of the angel who brought you here."

"So be it!"

The Capuchin made a slow gesture of benediction, and I bowed my head to receive it. After he left, I admit that I didn't feel like laughing. In a stupor, almost in fear, I noticed that a ring was missing from my finger which I had worn for many years and which I was accustomed to use as a seal. I couldn't recall where I had lost it. It was an antique ring. It had my escutcheon engraved in amethyst, and had belonged to my grandfather the Marquis of Bradomín.

I descended to the garden, where the swifts were flying in the blue shade of evening. The deep, silent paths lined with age-old myrtles resembled fanciful roads inviting meditation and forgetfulness, amid fresh aromas scattered in the breeze by the humble herbs that

---

12. Or: "local-style." Another Galicianism, and a somewhat ambiguous one.

brotaban escondidas como virtudes. Llegaba a mí sofocado y continuo el rumor de las fuentes sepultadas entre el verde perenne de los mirtos, de los laureles y de los bojes. Una vibración misteriosa parecía salir del jardín solitario, y un afán desconocido me oprimía el corazón. Yo caminaba bajo los cipreses, que dejaban caer de su cima un velo de sombra. Desde lejos, como a través de larga sucesión de pórticos, distinguí a María Rosario sentada al pie de una fuente, leyendo en un libro: Seguí andando con los ojos fijos en aquella feliz aparición. Al ruido de mis pasos alzó levemente la cabeza, y con dos rosas de fuego en las mejillas volvió a inclinarla, y continuó leyendo. Yo me detuve porque esperaba verla huir, y no encontraba las delicadas palabras que convenían a su gracia eucarística de lirio blanco. Al verla sentada al pie de la fuente, sobre aquel fondo de bojes antiguos, leyendo el libro abierto en sus rodillas, adiviné que María Rosario tenía por engaño del sueño, mi aparición en su alcoba. Al cabo de un momento volvió a levantar la cabeza, y sus ojos, en un batir de párpados, echaron sobre mí una mirada furtiva. Entonces le dije:

—¿Qué leéis en este retiro?

Sonrió tímidamente:

—La Vida de la Virgen María.

Tomé el libro de sus manos, y al cedérmelo, mientras una tenue llamarada encendía de nuevo sus mejillas, me advirtió:

—Tened cuidado que no caigan las flores disecadas que hay entre las páginas.

—No temáis . . .

Abrí el libro con religioso cuidado, aspirando la fragancia delicada y marchita que exhalaba como un aroma de santidad. En voz baja leí:

—«La Ciudad Mística de Sor María de Jesús, llamada de Ágreda.»

Volví a entregárselo, y ella, al recibirlo, interrogó sin osar mirarme:

—¿Acaso conocéis este libro?

—Lo conozco porque mi padre espiritual lo leía cuando estuvo prisionero en los Plomos de Venecia.

María Rosario, un poco confusa, murmuró:

—¡Vuestro padre espiritual! ¿Quién es vuestro padre espiritual?

—El Caballero de Casanova.

—¿Un noble español?

—No, un aventurero veneciano.

sprouted there, hidden like virtues. There came to me, muffled and
steady, the sound of the fountains buried amid the perennial green of
the myrtle, laurel, and box. A mysterious vibration seemed to issue
from the solitary garden, and an unfamiliar anguish oppressed my
heart. I was walking under the cypresses, which dropped a veil of
shadow from their tops. In the distance, as if across a long succession
of porticos, I could discern María Rosario seated at the foot of a fountain, reading a book. I kept going, my eyes fixed on that blissful ap-
parition. At the sound of my footsteps, she gently raised her head, and
with two fiery roses on her cheeks, let it fall again, and went on reading. I stopped because I hoped to see her flee and I couldn't find the
delicate words befitting her eucharistic grace, like a white lily's. Seeing
her seated at the foot of the fountain, against that backdrop of ancient
box trees, reading the book open on her knees, I guessed that María
Rosario thought my appearance in her bedroom had been the illusion
of a dream. After a moment she raised her head again, and her eyes,
in a beating of eyelids, cast a furtive glance at me. Then I said to her:

"What are you reading in this secluded spot?"

She smiled shyly:

"The life of the Virgin Mary."

I took the book from her hands, and on surrendering it to me, while
a slight blush reddened her cheeks again, she warned me:

"Be careful not to drop the dried flowers between the pages."

"Don't worry . . ."

I opened the book with religious care, inhaling the delicate fragrance of faded flowers which it emitted like the odor of sanctity. In
low tones I read:

"*The Mystical City* by Sister Mary of Jesus, called Mary of Ágreda."[13]

I handed it back to her, and when she took it she asked, not daring
to look at me:

"Do you know this book by any chance?"

"I know it because my spiritual father used to read it when a prisoner in the Leads in Venice."

María Rosario, somewhat confused, murmured:

"Your spiritual father? Who is your spiritual father?"

"The Chevalier Casanova."

"A Spanish nobleman?"

"No, a Venetian adventurer."

---

13. This unorthodox retelling of the life of the Virgin by the Venerable Mother María
de Jesús de Ágreda (1602–1665) was first published in Madrid in 1670 as *Mystica civ-
dad de Dios.* Though assailed by the hierarchy, it remained popular for centuries.

—¿Y un aventurero . . . ?

Yo la interrumpí:

—Se arrepintió al final de su vida.

—¿Se hizo fraile?

—No tuvo tiempo, aun cuando dejó escritas sus confesiones.

—¿Como San Agustín?

—¡Lo mismo! Pero humilde y cristiano, no quiso igualarse con aquel Doctor de la Iglesia, y las llamó Memorias.

—¿Vos las habéis leído?

—Es mi lectura favorita.

—¿Serán muy edificantes?

—¡Oh . . . ! ¡Cuánto aprenderíais en ellas . . . ! Jacobo de Casanova fue gran amigo de una monja de Venecia.

—¿Como San Francisco fue amigo de Santa Clara?

—Con una amistad todavía más íntima.

—¿Y cuál era la regla de la monja?

—Carmelita.

—Yo también seré Carmelita.

María Rosario calló ruborizándose, y quedó con los ojos fijos en el cristal de la fuente, que la reflejaba toda entera. Era una fuente rústica cubierta de musgo. Tenía un murmullo tímido como de plegaria, y estaba sepultada en el fondo de un claustro circular, formado por arcos de antiquísimos bojes. Yo me incliné sobre la fuente, y como si hablase con la imagen que temblaba en el cristal de agua, murmuré:

—¡Vos, cuando estéis en el convento, no seréis mi amiga . . . !

María Rosario se apartó vivamente:

—¡Callad . . . ! ¡Callad, os lo suplico . . . !

Estaba pálida, y juntaba las manos mirándome con sus hermosos ojos angustiados. Me sentí tan conmovido, que sólo supe inclinarme en demanda de perdón. Ella gimió:

—Callad, porque de otra suerte no podré deciros . . .

Se llevó las manos a la frente y estuvo así un instante. Yo veía que toda su figura temblaba. De repente, con una fuerza trágica se descubrió el rostro, y clamó enronquecida:

—¡Aquí vuestra vida peligra . . . ! ¡Salid hoy mismo!

Y corrió a reunirse con sus hermanas, que venían por una honda carrera de mirtos, las unas en pos de las otras, hablando y cogiendo flores para el altar de la capilla. Me alejé lentamente. Empezaba a declinar la tarde, y sobre la piedra de armas que coronaba la puerta del jardín, se arrullaban dos palomas que huyeron al acercarme.

"And an adventurer . . . ?"

I interrupted her:

"He repented at the end of his life."

"Did he become a friar?"

"He didn't have the time, even after he had finished writing his confessions."

"Like Saint Augustine?"

"Exactly! But being a humble Christian, he didn't want to place himself on the same footing as that Doctor of the Church, and he called them memoirs."

"You've read them?"

"They're my favorite book."

"They must be very edifying?"

"Oh! . . . How much you could learn from them! . . . Jacopo Casanova was a great friend of a Venetian nun."

"The way that Saint Francis was the friend of Saint Clare?"

"With a friendship even more intimate."

"And what rule did the nun follow?"

"Carmelite."

"I'll be a Carmelite, too."

María Rosario fell silent, blushing, and kept her gaze fixed on the glassy surface of the fountain, which reflected her entire person. It was a rustic, moss-covered fountain. It had a shy babble like a prayer, and was buried at the back of a circular cloister formed by arches of age-old box trees. I leaned over the fountain and, as if speaking to the image trembling on the watery surface, I whispered:

"When *you* are in the convent, you won't be my friend . . . !"

María Rosario moved away briskly:

"Be still! . . . Be still, I implore you! . . ."

She was pale, and she clasped her hands, looking at me with her lovely eyes in anguish. I felt so moved that all I could do was to bow as a request for forgiveness. She moaned:

"Be still, because otherwise I won't be able to tell you . . ."

She raised her hands to her forehead and remained that way for an instant. I saw that she was trembling all over. Suddenly, with a tragic force she uncovered her face and shouted hoarsely:

"Your life is in danger here! . . . Leave this very day!"

And she ran to rejoin her sisters, who were coming down a deep myrtle-lined path, some behind the others, chatting and picking flowers for the chapel altar. I moved away slowly. The afternoon was drawing to a close, and over the stone escutcheon that crowned the garden gate

Tenían adornado el cuello con alegres listones de seda, tal vez anudados un día por aquellas manos místicas y ardientes que sólo hicieron el bien sobre la tierra. Matas de viejos alelíes florecían en las grietas del muro, y los lagartos tomaban el sol sobre las piedras caldeadas, cubiertas de un liquen seco y amarillento. Abrí la cancela y quedé un momento contemplando aquel jardín lleno de verdor umbrío y de reposo señorial. El sol poniente dejaba un reflejo dorado sobre los cristales de una torre que aparecía cubierta de negros vencejos, y en el silencio de la tarde se oía el murmullo de las fuentes y las voces de las cinco hermanas.

Flanqueada la muralla del jardín, llegué a la casuca terreña que tenía la cornamenta de un buey en el tejado. Una vieja hilaba sentada en el quicio de la puerta, y por el camino pasaban rebaños de ovejas levantando nubes de polvo. La vieja al verme llegar, se puso en pie:

—¿Qué deseáis?

Y al mismo tiempo, con un gesto de bruja avarienta, humedecía en los labios decrépitos el dedo pulgar para seguir torciendo el lino. Yo le dije:

—Tengo que hablaros.

A la vista de dos sequines, la vieja sonrió agasajadora:

—¡Pasad . . . ! ¡Pasad . . . !

Dentro de la casa ya era completamente de noche, y la vieja tuvo que andar a tientas para encender un candil de aceite. Luego de colgarle en un clavo, volvióse a mí:

—¡Veamos qué desea tan gentil caballero!

Y sonreía mostrando la caverna desdentada de su boca. Yo hice un gesto indicándole que cerrase la puerta, y obedeció solícita, no sin echar antes una mirada al camino por donde un rebaño desfilaba tardo, al son de las esquilas. Después vino a sentarse en un taburete, debajo del candil, y me dijo juntando sobre el regazo las manos que parecían un haz de huesos:

—Por sabido tengo que estáis enamorado, y vuestra es la culpa si no sois feliz. Antes hubieseis venido, y antes tendríais el remedio.

Oyéndola hablar de esta suerte comprendí que se hacía pasar por hechicera, y no pude menos de sorprenderme, recordando las misteriosas palabras del capuchino. Quedé un momento silencioso, y la vieja, esperando mi respuesta, no me apartaba los ojos astutos y desconfiados. De pronto le grité:

two doves were cooing; they flew away when I approached. Their necks were adorned with jolly silk ribbons, perhaps knotted one day by those mystical, ardent hands which did nothing but good on earth. Clumps of old wallflowers blossomed in the cracks of the wall, and the lizards were basking in the sun on the sun-baked stones, which were covered with dry, yellowish lichen. I opened the gate and lingered a moment studying that garden full of shady greenery and stately repose. The setting sun was leaving a golden reflection on the glass panes of a tower that seemed covered with black swifts, and in the evening silence could be heard the murmuring of the fountains and the voices of the five sisters.

After turning the garden wall, I reached the earth-colored hut that had an ox's horns on its roof. An old woman was spinning as she sat in the door frame, and flocks of sheep passed down the road, raising clouds of dust. On seeing me arrive, the old woman stood up:

"What do you wish?"

And at the same time, with the gesture of a greedy witch, she moistened her thumb with her decrepit lips so she could continue to twist the flax. I said:

"I must talk to you."

At the sight of two zecchini, the old woman smiled hospitably:

"Come in . . . ! Come in . . . !"

Inside the house it was already completely dark, and the old woman had to grope around to light an oil lamp. After hanging it on a nail, she turned to me:

"Let's see what such a fine gentleman wishes!"

And she smiled, showing the toothless cavern of her mouth. I made a gesture indicating that she should lock the door and she obeyed readily, not without first casting a glance at the road, down which a flock was slowly passing, to the sound of their collar bells. Then she sat down on a stool, under the lamp, and joining her hands, which resembled a bundle of bones, on her lap, she said:

"I know for a fact that you're in love, and it's your fault if you're unhappy. You should have come sooner, and you'd have had the remedy sooner."

Hearing her speak that way, I understood that she passed herself off as a sorceress, and I couldn't help being surprised, remembering the Capuchin's mysterious words. I remained silent for a moment, and the old woman, awaiting my reply, never took her shrewd, distrustful eyes off me. All at once I shouted at her:

—Sabed, señora bruja, que tan sólo vengo por un anillo que me han robado.

La vieja se incorporó horriblemente demudada:

—¿Qué decís?

—Que vengo por mi anillo.

—¡No lo tengo! ¡Yo no os conozco!

Y quiso correr hacia la puerta para abrirla, pero yo le puse una pistola en el pecho, y retrocedió hacia un rincón dando suspiros. Entonces sin moverme le dije:

—Vengo dispuesto a daros doble dinero del que os han prometido por obrar el maleficio, y lejos de perder, ganaréis entregándome el anillo y cuanto os trajeron con él . . .

Se levantó del suelo todavía dando suspiros, y vino a sentarse en el taburete debajo del candil, que al oscilar, tan pronto dejaba toda la figura en la sombra, como iluminaba el pergamino del rostro y de las manos. Lagrimeando murmuró:

—Perderé cinco sequines, pero vos me daréis doble cuando sepáis . . . Porque acabo de reconoceros . . .

—Decid entonces quién soy.

—Sois un caballero español que sirve en la Guardia Noble del Santo Padre.

—¿No sabéis mi nombre?

—Sí, esperad . . .

Y quedó un momento con la cabeza inclinada, procurando acordarse. Yo veía temblar sobre sus labios palabras que no podían oírse. De pronto me dijo:

—Sois el Marqués de Bradomín.

Juzqué entonces que debía sacar de la bolsa los diez sequines prometidos y mostrárselos. La vieja entonces lloró enternecida:

—Excelencia, nunca os hubiera hecho morir, pero os hubiera quitado la lozanía . . .

—Explicadme eso.

—Venid conmigo . . .

Me hizo pasar tras un cañizo negro y derrengado, que ocultaba el hogar donde ahumaba una lumbre mortecina con olor de azufre. Yo confieso que sentía un vago sobresalto, ante los poderes misteriosos de la bruja, capaces de hacerme perder la lozanía.

La bruja había descolgado el candil: Alzábale sobre su cabeza para alumbrarse mejor, y me mostraba el fondo de su vivienda, que hasta

"I'll have you know, madam witch, that I've only come for a ring that's been stolen from me!"

The old woman sat up, her face horribly distorted:

"What's that you say?"

"That I've come for my ring."

"I don't have it! I don't know you!"

And she tried to run to the door to open it, but I set a pistol to her bosom, and she retreated to a corner, heaving sighs. Then, without budging, I said:

"I'm ready to offer you double the amount you've been promised to work the spell, and, far from losing, you'll gain more if you hand over to me the ring and everything else that was brought to you at the same time . . ."

She got up from the floor, still heaving sighs, and sat down on the stool under the lamp, which, as it swung, now left her entire figure in the dark, now lit up the parchment of her face and hands. Tearfully she murmured:

"I'll lose five zecchini, but you'll give me twice that when you find out . . . Because I've just recognized you . . ."

"Then tell me who I am."

"You're a Spanish gentleman serving in the Holy Father's noble guards."

"You don't know my name?"

"Yes, wait . . ."

And she remained for a moment with her head bowed, trying to remember. I saw words I couldn't hear trembling on her lips. All at once, she said:

"You're the Marquis of Bradomín."

Then I deemed that I ought to draw from my purse the ten zecchini I had promised, and to show them to her. Then the old woman wept with emotion:

"Excellency, I would never have caused your death, but I would have taken away your virility . . ."

"Explain that to me."

"Come with me . . ."

She had me pass behind a black, warped wattle screen that hid the hearth in which a dying fire was smoking with a sulphurous odor. I confess that I felt a vague alarm at the witch's mysterious powers, capable of depriving me of my manhood.

The witch had taken the lamp down from the nail. She was holding it over her head to cast more light on herself, and she was showing me

entonces, por estar entre sombras, no había podido ver. Al oscilar la luz, yo distinguía claramente sobre paredes negras de humo, lagartos, huesos puestos en cruz, piedras lucientes, clavos y tenazas. La bruja puso el candil en tierra y se agachó revolviendo en la ceniza:

—Ved aquí vuestro anillo.

Y lo limpió cuidadosamente en la falda, antes de dármelo, y quiso ella misma colocarlo en mi mano:

—¿Por qué os trajeron ese anillo?

—Para hacer el sortilegio era necesaria una piedra que llevaseis desde hacía muchos años.

—¿Y cómo me la robaron?

—Estando dormido, Excelencia.

—¿Y vos qué intentabais hacer?

—Ya antes os lo dije . . . Me mandaban privaros de toda vuestra fuerza viril . . . Hubierais quedado como un niño acabado de nacer . . .

—¿Cómo obraríais ese prodigio?

—Vais a verlo.

Siguió revolviendo en la ceniza y descubrió una figura de cera toda desnuda, acostada en el fondo del brasero. Aquel ídolo, esculpido sin duda por el mayordomo, tenía una grotesca semejanza conmigo. Mirándole, yo reía largamente, mientras la bruja rezongaba:

—¡Ahora os burláis! ¡Desgraciado de vos si hubiese bañado esa figura en sangre de mujer, según mi ciencia . . . ! ¡Y más desgraciado cuando la hubiese fundido en las brasas . . . !

—¿Era todo eso?

—Sí . . .

—Tened vuestros diez sequines. Ahora abrid la puerta.

La vieja me miró astuta:

—¿Ya os vais, Excelencia? ¿No deseáis nada de mí? Si me dais otros diez sequines, yo haré delirar por vuestros amores a la Señora Princesa. ¿No queréis, Excelencia?

Yo repuse secamente:

—No.

La vieja entonces tomó del suelo el candil, y abrió la puerta. Salí al camino, que estaba desierto. Era completamente de noche, y comenzaban a caer gruesas gotas de agua, que me hicieron apresurar el paso. Mientras me alejaba iba pensando en el reverendo capuchino que había tenido tan cabal noticia de todo aquello. Hallé cerrada la cancela del jardín y tuve que hacer un largo rodeo. Daban las nueve en el reloj de la Catedral cuando atravesaba el arco románico que conduce a la plaza donde se alza el Palacio Gaetani. Estaban iluminados los bal-

the far end of her dwelling, which I hadn't been able to see until then, since it had been in darkness. As the flame wavered, I could clearly discern on the smoke-blackened walls lizards, crossbones, gleaming stones, nails, and tongs. The witch set the lamp down on the floor and squatted, poking up the ashes:

"Here is your ring."

And she cleaned it carefully on her skirt before giving it to me. She insisted on placing it on my finger herself.

"Why was that ring brought to you?"

"To work the spell, I needed a stone you had worn for many years."

"And how was it stolen?"

"While you slept, Excellency."

"And what did you intend to do?"

"I've already told you . . . I was ordered to deprive you of all your manly powers . . . You would have been left like a new-born child . . ."

"How were you to accomplish that wonder?"

"You'll see."

She continued to poke up the ashes, and she uncovered a wax figure, completely nude, lying at the back of the hearth. That idol, no doubt modeled by the butler, bore a grotesque resemblance to me. Looking at it, I laughed for some time, while the witch was grumbling:

"Now you joke about it! Woe to you if I had washed that figure in women's blood according to my craft . . . ! And greater woe, once I had melted it in the embers . . . !"

"Was that all?"

"Yes . . ."

"Take your ten zecchini. Now unlock the door."

The old woman looked at me astutely:

"Going already, Excellency? You wish nothing from me? If you give me ten more zecchini, I'll make the princess go mad for love of you. Don't you want that, Excellency?"

I replied curtly:

"No."

Then the old woman lifted the lamp from the floor and opened the door. I emerged onto the road, which was empty. Night had fallen, and heavy drops of rain were beginning to fall, making me hasten my pace. As I came away, I kept thinking of the reverend Capuchin who had been so fully informed of all this. I found the garden gate locked and I had to make a long detour. The cathedral clock was striking nine when I passed through the Romanesque arch leading to the square on which the Gaetani palace stands. The balconies were illuminated, and

cones, y de la iglesia de los Dominicos salía entre cirios el Paso de la
Cena. Aún recuerdo aquellas procesiones largas, tristes, rumorosas,
que desfilaban en medio de grandes chubascos. Había procesiones al
rayar el día, y procesiones por la tarde, y procesiones a la media
noche. Las cofradías eran innumerables. Entonces la Semana Santa
tenía fama en aquella vieja ciudad pontificia.

La Princesa, durante la tertulia, no me habló ni me miró una sola
vez. Yo, temiendo que aquel desdén fuese advertido, decidí retirarme.
Con la sonrisa en los labios llegué hasta donde la noble señora hablaba
suspirando. Cogí audazmente su mano, y la besé, haciéndole sentir la
presión decidida y fuerte de mis labios. Vi palidecer intensamente sus
mejillas y brillar el odio en sus ojos, sin embargo, supe inclinarme con
galante rendimiento y solicitar su venia para retirarme. Ella repuso
fríamente:

—Eres dueño de hacer tu voluntad.

—¡Gracias, Princesa!

Salí del salón en medio de un profundo silencio. Sentíame humi-
llado, y comprendía que acababa de hacerse imposible mi estancia en
el Palacio. Pasé la noche en el retiro de la biblioteca, preocupado con
este pensamiento, oyendo batir monótonamente el agua en los
cristales de las ventanas. Sentíame presa de un afán doloroso y con-
tenido, algo que era insensata impaciencia de mí mismo, y de las
horas, y de todo cuanto me rodeaba. Veíame como prisionero en
aquella biblioteca oscura, y buscaba entrar en mi verdadera conciencia, para juzgar todo lo acaecido durante aquel día con serena y firme
reflexión. Quería resolver, quería decidir, y extraviábase mi pensamiento, y mi voluntad desaparecía, y todo esfuerzo era vano.

¡Fueron horas de tortura indefinible! Ráfagas de una insensata vio-
lencia agitaban mi alma. Con el vértigo de los abismos me atraían
aquellas asechanzas misteriosas, urdidas contra mí en la sombra perfumada de los grandes salones. Luchaba inútilmente por dominar mi
orgullo y convencerme que era más altivo y más gallardo abandonar
aquella misma noche, en medio de la tormenta, el Palacio Gaetani.
Advertíame presa de una desusada agitación, y al mismo tiempo comprendía que no era dueño de vencerla, y que todas aquellas larvas que
entonces empezaban a removerse dentro de mí, habían de ser fatal-
mente furias y sierpes. Con un presentimiento sombrío, sentía que mi
mal era incurable y que mi voluntad era impotente para vencer la

from the church of the Dominicans the tableau of the Last Supper emerged amid tapers. I still recall those long, sad, noisy processions which kept marching amid heavy showers. There were processions at dawn, processions in the afternoon, and processions at midnight. There were innumerable religious fraternities. In those days the Holy Week celebrations in that old papal city were famous.

During her regular salon gathering, the princess didn't speak to me or look at me once. Afraid that her contempt would be noticed, I decided to withdraw. A smile on my lips, I went up to where the noble lady was sighing as she spoke. I grasped her hand boldly and kissed it, making her feel the strong, determined pressure of my lips. I saw her cheeks turn deathly pale, while hatred gleamed in her eyes; nevertheless, I was able to bow with gallant submissiveness and beg her leave to retire. She answered coldly:

"You may do just as you wish."

"Thank you, princess!"

I left the salon amid a deep silence. I felt humiliated, and I realized that my further stay in the palace had just become impossible. I spent the night in the seclusion of the library, dwelling on that thought, listening to the monotonous patter of the rain on the window panes. I felt myself a prey to a painful, repressed anguish, something akin to a foolish impatience with myself, with the passing hours, and with my entire surroundings. I saw myself as a prisoner in that dark library, and I sought to regain my normal state of mind in order to think over everything that had occurred that day with calm, steady reflection. I wanted to come to a resolution, to a decision, but my thoughts were roaming, my willpower was vanishing, and all my efforts were in vain.

Those were hours of indefinable torment! Gusts of senseless violence were stirring my soul. With the dizziness of one who peers into abysses, I was drawn onward by those mysterious traps laid for me in the perfumed shade of those large salons. I was struggling in vain to control my pride and to persuade myself that it was a prouder and more valiant thing to leave the Gaetani palace that very night, in the middle of the storm. I noticed that I was prey to an unaccustomed agitation, and at the same time I realized that I was unable to subdue it, and that all those specters then beginning to stir within me simply had to be furies and serpents. With a somber foreboding, I felt that my ailment was incurable and that my will was powerless to overcome the

tentación de hacer alguna cosa audaz, irreparable. ¡Era aquello el vértigo de la perdición . . . !

A pesar de la lluvia, abrí la ventana. Necesitaba respirar el aire fresco de la noche. El cielo estaba negro. Una ráfaga aborrascada pasó sobre mi cabeza: Algunos pájaros sin nido habían buscado albergue bajo el alero, y con estremecimientos llenos de frío sacudían el plumaje mojado, piando tristemente. En la plaza resonaba la canturia de una procesión lejana. La iglesia del convento tenía las puertas abiertas, y en el fondo brillaba el altar iluminado. Oíase la voz senil de una carraca. Las devotas salían de la iglesia y se cobijaban bajo el arco de la plaza para ver llegar la procesión. Entre dos hileras de cirios bamboleaban las andas, allá en el confín de una calle estrecha y alta. En la plaza esperaban muchos curiosos cantando una oración rimada. La lluvia redoblando en los paraguas, y el chapoteo de los pies en las charcas contrastaban con la nota tibia y sensual de las enaguas blancas que asomaban bordeando los vestidos negros, como espumas que bordean sombrío oleaje de tempestad. Las dos señoras de los negros y crujientes vestidos de seda, salieron de la iglesia, y pisando en la punta de los pies, atravesaron corriendo la plaza, para ver la procesión desde las ventanas del Palacio. Una ráfaga agitaba sus mantos.

Caían gruesas gotas de agua que dejaban un lamparón oscuro en las losas de la plaza. Yo tenía las mejillas mojadas, y sentía como una vaga efusión de lágrimas. De pronto se iluminaron los balcones, y las Princesas, con otras damas, asomaron en ellos. Cuando la procesión llegaba bajo el arco, llovía a torrentes. Yo la vi desfilar desde el balcón de la biblioteca, sintiendo a cada instante en la cara el salpicar de la lluvia arremolinada por el viento. Pasaron primero los Hermanos del Calvario, silenciosos y encapuchados. Después los Hermanos de la Pasión, con hopas amarillas y cirios en las manos. Luego seguían los pasos: Jesús en el Huerto de las Olivas, Jesús ante Pilatos, Jesús ante Herodes, Jesús atado a la columna. Bajo aquella lluvia fría y cenicienta tenían una austeridad triste y desolada. El último en aparecer fue el Paso de las Caídas. Sin cuidarse del agua, las damas se arrastraron de rodillas hasta la balaustrada del balcón. Oyóse la voz trémula del mayordomo:

—¡Ya llega! ¡Ya llega!

Llegaba, sí, pero cuán diferente de como lo habíamos visto la primera vez en una sala del Palacio. Los cuatro judíos habían depuesto su fiereza, bajo la lluvia. Sus cabezas de cartón se despintaban. Ablandábanse los cuerpos, y flaqueaban las piernas como si fuesen a hincarse de rodillas. Parecían arrepentidos. Las dos hermanas de

temptation to do something rash, irreparable. That was the dizziness of perdition! . . .

Despite the rain I opened the window. I had to breathe the cool night air. The sky was black. A stormy gust blew over my head. A few birds without nests had sought shelter under the eaves, and shivering with the cold, they were shaking out their wet feathers, chirping sadly. In the square could be heard the chanting of a distant procession. The convent church had its doors open, and in the back the lighted altar was shining. The senile voice of a decrepit old woman was heard. The female devotees were leaving the church and taking shelter under the arch beside the square to watch the procession arrive. Between the rows of tapers the platform was rocking, at the end of a narrow, high street. In the square many onlookers were waiting, singing a rhymed prayer. The rain drumming on the umbrellas and the splashing of feet in puddles were a contrast to the warm, sensual note of the white petticoats that peeped out under the hems of the black dresses, like foam edging the dark surf of a stormy sea. The two ladies in black, rustling silk dresses came out of the church and on tiptoe crossed the square at a run, to watch the procession from the palace windows. A gust was stirring their capes.

Heavy raindrops were falling and leaving a dark stain on the paving stones of the square. My cheeks were wet, and I seemed to feel a vague effusion of tears. Suddenly the balconies were lighted up, and the princesses, with other ladies, appeared on them. When the procession arrived under the archway, it was raining torrentially. I watched it march by from the library balcony, all the while feeling on my face the sprinkling of the rain whirled about by the wind. First the Brothers of Calvary passed, silent, wearing hoods. Then the Brothers of the Passion, in yellow robes with tapers in their hands. Then followed the tableau platforms: Jesus on the Mount of Olives, Jesus before Pilate, Jesus before Herod, Jesus bound to the column. Beneath that cold, ashen rain, they had a sad, desolate austerity. The last to appear was the tableau of the Way of the Cross. Disregarding the rain, the ladies crept on their knees up to the balcony railing. The butler's shaky voice was heard:

"It's coming! It's coming!"

Yes, it was coming, but how differently from the way we had first seen it in a room in the palace! The four Jews had lost their ferocity in the rain. The colors on their cardboard heads were running. Their bodies were sagging, and their legs buckling, as if they were about to kneel down. They seemed repentant. The two sisters in the old-

los rancios vestidos de gro, viendo en ello un milagro, repetían llenas de unción:

—¡Edificante, Antonina!

—¡Edificante, Lorencina!

La lluvia caía sin tregua como un castigo, y desde un balcón frontero llegaban, con vaguedad de poesía y de misterio, los arrullos de dos tórtolas que cuidaba una vieja enlutada y consumida que rezaba entre dos cirios encendidos en altos candeleros, tras los cristales. Busqué con los ojos al Señor Polonio: Había desaparecido.

Poco después, apesadumbrado y dolorido, meditaba en mi cámara cuando una mano batió con los artejos en la puerta y la voz cascada del mayordomo vino a sacarme un momento del penoso cavilar:

—Excelencia, este pliego de Roma.

—¿Quién lo ha traído?

—Un correo que acaba de llegar.

Abrí el pliego y pasé por él una mirada. Monseñor Sassoferrato me ordenaba presentarme en Roma. Sin acabar de leerlo me volví al mayordomo, mostrando un profundo desdén:

—Señor Polonio, que dispongan mi silla de posta.

El mayordomo preguntó hipócritamente:

—¿Vais a partir, Excelencia?

—Antes de una hora.

—¿Lo sabe mi señora la Princesa?

—Vos cuidaréis de decírselo.

—¡Muy honrado, Excelencia! Ya sabéis que el postillón está enfermo . . . Habrá que buscar otro. Si me autorizáis para ello yo me encargo de hallar uno que os deje contento.

La voz del viejo y su mirada esquiva, despertaron en mi alma una sospecha. Juzgué que era temerario confiarse a tal hombre, y le dije:

—Yo veré a mi postillón.

Me hizo una profunda reverencia, y quiso retirarse, pero le detuve:

—Escuchad, Señor Polonio.

—Mandad, Excelencia.

Y cada vez se inclinaba con mayor respeto. Yo le clavé los ojos, mirándole en silencio: Me pareció que no podía dominar su inquietud. Adelantando un paso le dije:

—Como recuerdo de mi visita, quiero que conservéis esta piedra.

Y sonriendo me saqué de la mano aquel anillo, que tenía en una

fashioned grosgrain dresses, seeing a miracle in this, were repeating unctuously:

"Edifying, Antonina!"

"Edifying, Lorenzina!"

The rain was falling without letup, like a castigation, and from a balcony opposite, with the vagueness of poetry and mystery, came the cooing of two turtledoves kept by a withered old woman in mourning who was praying between two lighted tapers in tall candlesticks, behind the windows. I looked for Master Polonio. He had vanished.

Shortly afterward, gloomy and aggrieved, I was meditating in my room when there was a rap of knuckles at the door and the cracked voice of the butler jolted me out of my painful thoughts for a moment:

"Excellency, this message from Rome."

"Who brought it?"

"A courier who has just arrived."

I opened the missive and cast a glance at it. Monsignor Sassoferrato was ordering me to present myself in Rome. Without reading it to the end, I turned to the butler, manifesting deep contempt:

"Master Polonio, have my post chaise made ready."

The butler asked hypocritically:

"Are you leaving, Excellency?"

"In less than an hour!"

"Does my lady the princess know?"

"You will see to telling her."

"A great honor, Excellency! I'm sure you know the driver is ill . . . It will be necessary to get another one. If you give me leave to do so, I undertake to find one who will give you satisfaction."

The old man's voice and his disdainful gaze aroused a suspicion in my mind. I considered it foolhardy to trust such a man, and I said:

"I'll visit my driver."

He made me a low bow, and made to withdraw, but I detained him:

"Listen, Master Polonio."

"At your orders, Excellency."

And each time he bowed with greater respect. I stared at him, watching him silently. He seemed unable to control his nervousness. Taking a step forward, I said:

"As a souvenir of my visit, I want you to keep this stone."

And with a smile I drew from my finger that ring, which had my es-

amatista grabadas mis armas. El mayordomo me miró con ojos extraviados:

—¡Perdonad!

Y sus manos agitadas rechazaban el anillo. Yo insistí:

—Tomadlo.

Inclinó la cabeza y lo recibió temblando. Con un gesto imperioso le señalé la puerta:

—Ahora, salid.

El mayordomo llegó al umbral, y murmuró resuelto y acobardado:

—Guardad vuestro anillo.

Con insolencia de criado lo arrojó sobre una mesa. Yo le miré amenazador:

—Presumo que vais a salir por la ventana, Señor Polonio.

Retrocedió, gritando con energía:

—¡Conozco vuestro pensamiento! No basta a vuestra venganza el maleficio con que habéis deshecho aquellos judíos, obra de mis manos, y con ese anillo queréis embrujarme. ¡Yo haré que os delaten al Santo Oficio!

Y huyó de mi presencia haciendo la señal de la cruz como si huyese del Diablo. No pude menos de reírme largamente. Llamé a Musarelo, y le ordené que se enterase del mal que aquejaba al postillón. Pero Musarelo había bebido tanto, que no estaba capaz para cumplir mi mandato. Sólo pude averiguar que el postillón y Musarelo habían cenado con el Señor Polonio.

Qué triste es para mí el recuerdo de aquel día. María Rosario estaba en el fondo de un salón llenando de rosas los floreros de la capilla. Cuando yo entré, quedóse un momento indecisa: Sus ojos miraron medrosos hacia la puerta, y luego se volvieron a mí con un ruego tímido y ardiente. Llenaba en aquel momento el último florero, y sobre sus manos deshojóse una rosa. Yo entonces le dije, sonriendo:

—¡Hasta las rosas se mueren por besar vuestras manos!

Ella también sonrió contemplando las hojas que había entre sus dedos, y después con leve soplo las hizo volar. Quedamos silenciosos: Era la caída de la tarde y el sol doraba una ventana con sus últimos reflejos: Los cipreses del jardín levantaban sus cimas pensativas en el azul del crepúsculo, al pie de la vidriera iluminada. Dentro, apenas si se distinguía la forma de las cosas, y en el recogimiento del salón las rosas esparcían un perfume tenue y las palabras morían lentamente igual que la tarde. Mis ojos buscaban los ojos de María Rosario con el

cutcheon engraved on an amethyst. The butler looked at me with vacant eyes:

"Excuse me!"

And his fluttering hands rejected the ring. I insisted:

"Take it."

He bowed his head and received it, trembling. With an imperious
gesture I showed him the door:

"Now go."

The butler reached the threshold, and murmured resolutely,
though intimidated:

"Keep your ring."

With a servant's insolence he threw it onto a table. I looked at him
menacingly:

"I imagine you're going to leave by way of the window, Master Polonio."

He retreated, shouting energetically:

"I know what you're thinking! Your revenge isn't satisfied with the
spell that you used to dissolve those Jews, my creation; with this ring
you want to bewitch me. I'll have you reported to the Inquisition!"

And he fled from my presence, making the sign of the cross, as if
fleeing from the devil. I couldn't help indulging in a long laugh. I
called Musarello and ordered him to find out just what was wrong
with the chaise driver. But Musarello was so drunk that he was unable
to carry out my orders. All I could ascertain was that the driver and
Musarello had had supper with Master Polonio.

How sad for me is the memory of that day! María Rosario was at the
far end of a salon, filling the chapel vases with roses. When I came in,
she remained undecided for a moment. Her eyes looked fearfully at
the door, then turned back to me with a shy but ardent prayer. At that
moment she was filling the last vase, and the petals of one rose fell
onto her hands. I then said to her with a smile:

"Even the roses are dying to kiss your hands!"

She smiled, too, studying the petals she had between her fingers;
then with a light puff she sent them flying. We kept silent. Evening
was falling and the sun was gilding a window with its last beams. The
cypresses in the garden were raising their pensive tops into the blue
of the twilight, at the foot of the illuminated window. Inside, the shape
of things could barely be made out, and in the seclusion of the salon
the roses emitted a delicate fragrance and words died away as slowly
as the afternoon. My eyes sought María Rosario's eyes with the inten-

empeño de aprisionarlos en la sombra. Ella suspiró angustiada como si el aire le faltase, y apartándose el cabello de la frente con ambas manos, huyó hacia la ventana. Yo, temeroso de asustarla, no intenté seguirla y sólo le dije después de un largo silencio:

—¿No me daréis una rosa?

Volvióse lentamente y repuso con voz tenue:

—Si la queréis . . .

Dudó un instante, y de nuevo se acercó. Procuraba mostrarse serena, pero yo veía temblar sus manos sobre los floreros, al elegir la rosa. Con una sonrisa llena de angustia me dijo:

—Os daré la mejor.

Ella seguía buscando en los floreros. Yo suspiré romántico:

—La mejor está en vuestros labios.

Me miró apartándose pálida y angustiada:

—No sois bueno . . . ¿Por qué me decís esas cosas?

—Por veros enojada.

—¿Y eso os agrada? ¡Algunas veces me parecéis el Demonio . . . !

—El Demonio no sabe querer.

Quedóse silenciosa. Apenas podía distinguirse su rostro en la tenue claridad del salón, y sólo supe que lloraba cuando estallaron sus sollozos. Me acerqué queriendo consolarla:

—¡Oh . . . ! Perdonadme.

Y mi voz fue tierna, apasionada y sumisa. Yo mismo, al oírla, sentí su extraño poder de seducción. Era llegado el momento supremo, y presintiéndolo, mi corazón se estremecía con el ansia de la espera cuando está próxima una gran aventura. María Rosario cerraba los ojos con espanto, como al borde de un abismo. Su boca descolorida parecía sentir una voluptuosidad angustiosa. Yo cogí sus manos que estaban yertas: Ella me las abandonó sollozando, con un frenesí doloroso:

—¿Por qué os gozáis en hacerme sufrir . . . ? ¡Si sabéis que todo es imposible!

—¡Imposible . . . ! Yo nunca esperé conseguir vuestro amor . . . ¡Ya sé que no lo merezco . . . ! Solamente quiero pediros perdón y oír de vuestros labios que rezaréis por mí cuando esté lejos.

—¡Callad . . . ! ¡Callad . . . !

—Os contemplo tan alta, tan lejos de mí, tan ideal, que juzgo vuestras oraciones como las de una santa.

—¡Callad . . . ! ¡Callad . . . !

—Mi corazón agoniza sin esperanza. Acaso podré olvidaros, pero este amor habrá sido para mí como un fuego purificador.

tion of imprisoning them in the shadow. She gave an anguished sigh as if her breath failed her, and, brushing the hair off her brow with both hands, she fled to the window. Afraid of frightening her, I made no attempt to follow her, merely saying after a long silence:

"Won't you give me a rose?"

She turned slowly and replied in a ghost of a voice:

"If you want . . ."

She hesitated an instant, then approached me again. She was trying to look calm, but I could see her hands trembling over the vases as she selected a rose. With an anguish-filled smile she said:

"I'll give you the best one."

She kept searching in the vases. I sighed romantically:

"The best one is on your lips."

Drawing away, pale and distressed, she looked at me:

"You aren't kind . . . Why do you say such things to me?"

"To see you get angry."

"And you find that pleasant? Sometimes I think you're the devil . . . !"

"The devil doesn't know how to love."

She remained silent. I could hardly make out her face in the scanty light of the salon, and I only realized she was crying when she burst into sobs. I went up to her, trying to comfort her:

"Oh! . . . Forgive me!"

And my voice was tender, impassioned, and submissive. Hearing it, even I felt its strange power of seduction. The supreme moment had come and, foreseeing this, my heart was trembling with the anxiety of expectation one feels when a great adventure is at hand. María Rosario's eyes were shut with fright, as if she were on the brink of a precipice. Her bloodless lips seemed to feel an oppressive voluptuousness. I grasped her hands, which were rigid. She abandoned them to me with a sob, with a painful frenzy:

"Why do you enjoy making me suffer? . . . Since you know it's all impossible!"

"Impossible! . . . I never expected to win your love . . . Now I know that I don't deserve it! . . . I only want to beg your forgiveness and hear from your lips that you will pray for me when I'm far away."

"Be still! . . . Be still! . . ."

"I see you at such a height, so remote from me, such an ideal figure, that I look upon your prayers as those of a saint."

"Be still! . . . Be still! . . ."

"My heart is agonizing without hope. Perhaps I can forget you, but this love will have been for me like a purifying fire."

—¡Callad . . . ! ¡Callad . . . !

Yo tenía lágrimas en los ojos, y sabía que cuando se llora, las manos pueden arriesgarse a ser audaces. ¡Pobre María Rosario, quedóse pálida como una muerta, y pensé que iba a desmayarse en mis brazos! Aquella niña era una santa, y viéndome a tal extremo desgraciado, no tenía valor para mostrarse más cruel conmigo. Cerraba los ojos, y gemía agoniada:

—¡Dejadme . . . ! ¡Dejadme . . . !

Yo murmuré:

—¿Por qué me aborrecéis tanto?

—¡Porque sois el Demonio!

Me miró despavorida, como si al sonido de mi voz se despertase, y arrancándose de mis brazos huyó hacia la ventana que doraban todavía los últimos rayos del sol. Apoyó la frente en los cristales y comenzó a sollozar. En el jardín se levantaba el canto de un ruiseñor, que evocaba, en la sombra azul de la tarde, un recuerdo ingenuo de santidad.

María Rosario llamó a la más niña de sus hermanas, que, con una muñeca en brazos, acababa de asomar en la puerta del salón. La llamaba con un afán angustioso y poderoso que encendía el candor de su carne con divinas rosas:

—¡Entra . . . ! ¡Entra . . . !

La llamaba tendiéndole los brazos desde el fondo de la ventana. La niña, sin moverse, le mostró la muñeca.

—Me la hizo Polonio.

—Ven a enseñármela.

—¿No la ves así?

—No, no la veo.

María Nieves acabó por decidirse, y entró corriendo: Los cabellos flotaban sobre su espalda como una nube de oro. Era llena de gentileza, con movimientos de pájaro, alegres y ligeros: María Rosario, viéndola llegar, sonreía, cubierto el rostro de rubor y sin secar las lágrimas. Inclinóse para besarla, y la niña se le colgó al cuello, hablándole con agasajo al oído:

—¡Si le hicieses un vestido a mi muñeca!

—¿Cómo lo quieres . . . ?

María Rosario le acariciaba los cabellos, reteniéndola a su lado. Yo veía cómo sus dedos trémulos desaparecían bajo la infantil y olorosa crencha. En voz baja le dije:

"Be still! . . . Be still! . . ."

I had tears in my eyes, and I knew that when a man cries, his hands can take the risk of being bold. Poor María Rosario! She remained as pale as a corpse, and I thought she was going to faint away in my arms! That girl was a saint, and seeing me unfortunate to such an extent, she didn't have the heart to act more cruel to me. Her eyes were closed, and she was moaning in agony:

"Let me alone! . . . Let me alone! . . ."

I whispered:

"Why do you loathe me so?"

"Because you're the devil!"

She looked at me, terrified, as if waking up at the sound of my voice, and, tearing herself from my arms, she fled to the window, which the last sunbeams were still gilding. She leaned her brow against the panes and began to sob. In the garden there arose the song of a nightingale, which, in the blue shade of the evening, evoked a naïve memory of sainthood.

María Rosario called to her youngest sister, who, with a doll in her arms, had just appeared in the doorway to the salon. She called her with a powerful, oppressive anguish which reddened the whiteness of her skin with divine roses:

"Come in! . . . Come in! . . ."

She called her, holding out her arms from the window recess. The child, not moving from the spot, showed her the doll.

"Polonio made it for me."

"Come show it to me."

"Can't you see it from here?"

"No, I can't."

María Nieves finally made up her mind, and ran in. Her hair floated down her back like a golden cloud. She was full of gracefulness, her movements like a bird's, merry and delicate. María Rosario, seeing her come, smiled, her face all flushed, her tears undried. She stooped down to kiss her, and the child clung to her neck, speaking into her ear warmly:

"Could you make a dress for my doll?"

"What type would you like? . . ."

María Rosario was caressing her hair, keeping her beside her. I watched her trembling fingers disappearing in the child's fragrant mop of hair. In low tones I said to her:

—¿Qué temíais de mí?

Sus mejillas llamearon:

—Nada . . .

Y aquellos ojos como no he visto otros hasta ahora, ni los espero ver ya, tuvieron para mí una mirada tímida y amante. Callábamos conmovidos, y la niña empezó a referirnos la historia de su muñeca: Se llamaba Yolanda, y era una reina. Cuando le hiciesen aquel vestido de tisú, le pondrían también una corona. María Nieves hablaba sin descanso: Sonaba su voz con murmullo alegre, continuo, como el borboteo de una fuente. Recordaba cuántas muñecas había tenido, y quería contar la historia de todas: Unas habían sido reinas, otras pastoras. Eran largas historias confusas, donde se repetían continuamente las mismas cosas. La niña extraviábase en aquellos relatos como en el jardín encantado del ogro las tres niñas hermanas, Andara, Magalona y Aladina . . . De pronto huyó de nuestro lado. María Rosario la llamó sobresaltada:

—¡Ven . . . ! ¡No te vayas!

—No me voy.

Corría por el salón y la cabellera de oro le revoloteaba sobre los hombros. Como cautivos, la seguían a todas partes los ojos de María Rosario: Volvió a suplicarle:

—¡No te vayas . . . !

—Si no me voy.

La niña hablaba desde el fondo oscuro del salón. María Rosario, aprovechando el instante, murmuró con apagado acento:

—Marqués, salid de Ligura . . .

—¡Sería renunciar a veros!

—¿Y acaso no es hoy la última vez? Mañana entraré en el convento. ¡Marqués, oíd mi ruego!

—Quiero sufrir aquí . . . Quiero que mis ojos, que no lloran nunca, lloren cuando os vistan el hábito, cuando os corten los cabellos, cuando las rejas se cierren ante vos. ¡Quién sabe, si al veros sagrada por los votos, mi amor terreno no se convertirá en una devoción! ¡Vos sois una santa . . . !

—¡Marqués, no digáis impiedades!

Y me clavó los ojos tristes, suplicantes, guarnecidos de lágrimas como de oraciones purísimas. Entonces ya parecía olvidada de la niña que, sentada en un canapé, adormecía a su muñeca con viejas tonadillas del tiempo de las abuelas. En la sombra de aquel vasto salón donde las rosas esparcían su aroma, la canción de la niña tenía el

"What do you fear from me?"

Her cheeks burned:

"Nothing . . ."

And those eyes, the like of which I've never seen again, nor ever expect to see, gave me a shy, loving glance. We were silent in our emotion, and the child began to tell us the history of her doll. Her name was Yolanda, and she was a queen. Whenever that lamé dress was made for her, she would also be crowned. María Nieves chattered without letup. Her voice poured out in a continuous cheerful murmur, like the bubbling of a fountain. She mentioned every doll she had ever had, and wanted to tell the story of each one. Some had been queens; others, shepherdesses. The stories were long and confused, the same things being repeated over and over. The child was losing her way in those narratives just as the three little sisters Andara, Magalona, and Aladina lost their way in the ogre's enchanted garden . . . Suddenly she ran away from us. María Rosario called her with a start:

"Come back! . . . Don't go!"

"I'm not going."

She ran through the salon and her golden hair fluttered about her shoulders. As if held captive, María Rosario's eyes followed her everywhere. She implored her again:

"Don't go! . . ."

"You see I'm not going!"

The child was speaking form the dark far end of the salon. María Rosario, taking advantage of the moment, whispered in hushed tones:

"Marquis, leave Ligura! . . ."

"That would mean giving up seeing you!"

"And isn't today the last time, anyway? Tomorrow I shall enter the convent. Marquis, hear my prayer!"

"I want to suffer here . . . I want my eyes, which never weep, to weep when you are clothed in the habit, when your hair is clipped, when the iron grilles close in front of you. Who knows whether, on seeing you consecrated by your vows, my worldly love may not be converted into a religious devotion! You are a saint! . . ."

"Marquis, don't say impious things!"

And she fastened on me her sad, beseeching eyes, bejeweled with tears as if with the purest of prayers. By that time she seemed to have forgotten the child, who, seated on a settee, was singing her doll to sleep with old tunes from our grandmothers' days. In the darkness of that vast salon, in which the roses were shedding their fragrance, the girl's song

encanto de esas rancias galanterías que parece se hayan desvanecido con los últimos sones de un minué.

Como una flor de sensitiva, María Rosario temblaba bajo mis ojos. Yo adivinaba en sus labios el anhelo y el temor de hablarme. De pronto me miró ansiosa, parpadeando como si saliese de un sueño. Con los brazos tendidos hacia mí, murmuró arrebatada, casi violenta:

—Salid hoy mismo para Roma. Os amenaza un peligro y tenéis que defenderos. Habéis sido delatado al Santo Oficio.

Yo repetí, sin ocultar mi sorpresa:

—¿Delatado al Santo Oficio?

—Sí, por brujo . . . Vos habíais perdido un anillo, y por arte diabólica lo recobrasteis . . . ¡Eso dicen, Marqués!

Yo exclamé con ironía:

—¿Y quien lo dice es vuestra madre?

—¡No . . . !

Sonreí tristemente:

—¡Vuestra madre, que me aborrece porque vos me amáis . . . !

—¡Jamás . . . ! ¡Jamás . . . !

—¡Pobre niña, vuestro corazón tiembla por mí, presiente los peligros que me cercan, y quiere prevenirlos!

—¡Callad, por compasión . . . ! ¡No acuséis a mi madre . . . !

—¿Acaso ella no llevó su crueldad hasta acusaros a vos misma? ¿Acaso creyó vuestras palabras cuando le jurabais que no me habíais visto una noche?

—¡Sí, las creyó!

María Rosario había dejado de temblar. Erguíase inmaculada y heroica, como las santas ante las fieras del Circo. Yo insistí, con triste acento, gustando el placer doloroso y supremo del verdugo:

—No, no fuisteis creída. Vos lo sabéis. ¡Y cuántas lágrimas han vertido en la oscuridad vuestros ojos!

María Rosario retrocedió hasta el fondo de la ventana:

—¡Sois brujo . . . ! ¡Han dicho la verdad . . . ! ¡Sois brujo . . . !

Luego, rehaciéndose, quiso huir, pero yo la detuve:

—Escuchadme.

Ella me miraba con los ojos extraviados, haciendo la señal de la cruz:

—¡Sois brujo . . . ! ¡Por favor, dejadme!

Yo murmuré con desesperación:

possessed the enchantment of those gallant ways of yesteryear which
seem to have vanished along with the last notes of a minuet.

Like a mimosa blossom, María Rosario was trembling in my sight. I
could sense on her lips her longing to speak to me and her fear to do
so. Suddenly she looked at me in anxiety, blinking as if emerging from
a dream. Her arms held out to me, she whispered ecstatically, almost
violently:

"Leave for Rome this very day! A danger threatens you and you
must defend yourself. You've been reported to the Inquisition."

I repeated, unable to conceal my surprise:

"Reported to the Inquisition?"

"Yes, as a wizard . . . You had lost a ring, and you regained it by di-
abolical arts . . . That's what they say, marquis!"

I exclaimed with irony:

"And it's your mother who says so?"

"No! . . ."

I smiled sadly:

"Your mother, who loathes me because you love me! . . ."

"Never! . . . Never! . . ."

"Poor girl, your heart trembles for me, foreseeing the perils that
surround me and desiring to forestall them!"

"Be still, for pity's sake! . . . Don't accuse my mother! . . ."

"And hasn't she been so cruel as to accuse you yourself? And did
she believe your words when you swore you hadn't seen me on a certain night?"

"Yes, she believed them!"

María Rosario had ceased trembling. She rose to her full height,
immaculate and heroic, like the female saints who faced wild beasts in
the arena. I insisted, in doleful tones, tasting the supreme, sorrowful
pleasure of an executioner:

"No, you weren't believed. You know it. And how many tears your
eyes have shed in the darkness!"

María Rosario recoiled to the window recess:

"You *are* a wizard! . . . They told the truth! . . . You *are* a wizard! . . ."

Then, recovering, she tried to flee, but I detained her:

"Listen to me!"

She was looking at me with vacant eyes, making the sign of the cross:

"You *are* a wizard! . . . Please let me alone!"

I murmured in desperation:

—¿También vos me acusáis?

—Decid entonces, ¿cómo habéis sabido . . . ?

La miré largo rato en silencio, hasta que sentí descender sobre mi espíritu el numen sagrado de los profetas:

—Lo he sabido, porque habéis rezado mucho para que lo supiese . . . ¡He tenido en un sueño la revelación de todo . . . !

María Rosario respiraba anhelante. Otra vez quiso huir, y otra vez la detuve. Desfallecida y resignada, miró hacia el fondo del salón, llamando a la niña:

—¡Ven, hermana . . . ! ¡Ven!

Y le tendía los brazos: La niña acudió corriendo: María Rosario la estrechó contra su pecho alzándola del suelo, pero estaba tan desfallecida de fuerzas, que apenas podía sostenerla, y suspirando con fatiga tuvo que sentarla sobre el alféizar de la ventana. Los rayos del sol poniente circundaron como una aureola la cabeza infantil: La crencha sedeña y olorosa fue como onda de luz sobre los hombros de la niña. Yo busqué en la sombra la mano de María Rosario.

—¡Curadme . . . !

Ella murmuró retirándose:

—¿Y cómo . . . ?

—Jurad que me aborrecéis.

—Eso no . . .

—¿Y amarme?

—Tampoco. ¡Mi amor no es de este mundo!

Su voz era tan triste al pronunciar estas palabras, que yo sentí una emoción voluptuosa como si cayese sobre mi corazón rocío de lágrimas purísimas. Inclinándome para beber su aliento y su perfume, murmuré en voz baja y apasionada:

—Vos me pertenecéis. Hasta la celda del convento os seguirá mi culto mundano. Solamente por vivir en vuestro recuerdo y en vuestras oraciones, moriría gustoso.

—¡Callad . . . ! ¡Callad . . . !

María Rosario, con el rostro intensamente pálido, tendía sus manos temblorosas hacia la niña, que estaba sobre el alféizar, circundada por el último resplandor de la tarde, como un arcángel en una vidriera antigua. El recuerdo de aquel momento aún pone en mis mejillas un frío de muerte. Ante nuestros ojos espantados se abrió la ventana, con ese silencio de las cosas inexorables que están determinadas en lo invisible y han de suceder por un destino fatal y cruel. La figura de la niña, inmóvil sobre el alféizar, se destacó un momento en el azul del cielo

"You, too, accuse me?"

"Then tell me how you knew . . ."

I looked at her in silence for some time, until I felt the sacred numen of the prophets descending onto my spirit:

"I knew it because you said many prayers to have me know it . . . I had a revelation of the whole thing in a dream! . . ."

María Rosario was breathing heavily. Once again she tried to flee, and once again I detained her. Weak and resigned, she gazed at the far end of the salon, calling the child:

"Come, sister! . . . Come!"

And she held out her arms to her. The child came running. María Rosario hugged her to her bosom, lifting her off the ground, but her strength had so given out that she could hardly support her, and sighing with fatigue, she was forced to seat her on the sill of the window. The beams of the setting sun encircled the child's head like an aureole. Her silky, fragrant hair was like a billow of light on the child's shoulders. I sought María Rosario's hand in the dark.

"Cure me! . . ."

Withdrawing, she murmured:

"How?"

"Swear that you hate me."

"I don't . . ."

"Do you love me, then?"

"Not that, either. My love is not of this world!"

Her voice was so sad when she uttered those words that I felt a voluptuous sensation, as if the dew of very pure tears had fallen on my heart. Stooping over to drink in her breath and her fragrance, I whispered in a low, impassioned tone:

"You belong to me. My worldly worship will follow you to your very cell in the convent. If I could only live in your memory and in your prayers, I'd gladly die."

"Be still! . . . Be still! . . ."

María Rosario, her face extremely pale, held out her trembling hands to the child, who was on the sill, environed by the final glow of sunset, like an archangel in an old stained-glass window. The recollection of that moment still casts a deathly chill on my cheeks. Before our terrified eyes the window opened, with the silence of inexorable things that are resolved upon in invisible space and happen of necessity through a fatal, cruel destiny. The child's figure, motionless on the sill, was outlined for a moment against the blue of the sky, in which

donde palidecían las estrellas, y cayó al jardín, cuando llegaban a tocarla los brazos de la hermana.

¡Fue Satanás! ¡Fue Satanás . . . ! Aún resuena en mi oído aquel grito angustiado de María Rosario: Después de tantos años aún la veo pálida, divina y trágica como el mármol de una estatua antigua: Aún siento el horror de aquella hora:

—¡Fue Satanás . . . ! ¡Fue Satanás . . . !

La niña estaba inerte sobre el borde de la escalinata. El rostro aparecía entre el velo de los cabellos blanco como un lirio, y de la rota sien manaba el hilo de sangre que los iba empapando. La hermana, como una poseída, gritaba:

—¡Fue Satanás . . . ! ¡Fue Satanás . . . !

Levanté a la niña en brazos y sus ojos se abrieron un momento llenos de tristeza. La cabeza ensangrentada y mortal rodó yerta sobre mi hombro, y los ojos se cerraron de nuevo lentos como dos agonías. Los gritos de la hermana resonaban en el silencio del jardín:

—¡Fue Satanás . . . ! ¡Fue Satanás . . . !

La cabellera de oro, aquella cabellera fluida como la luz, olorosa como un huerto, estaba negra de sangre. Yo la sentí pesar sobre mi hombro semejante a la fatalidad en un destino trágico. Con la niña en brazos subí la escalinata. En lo alto salió a mi encuentro el coro angustiado de las hermanas. Yo escuché su llanto y sus gritos, yo sentí la muda interrogación de aquellos rostros pálidos que tenían el espanto en los ojos. Los brazos se tendían hacia mí desesperados, y ellos recogieron el cuerpo de la hermana, y lo llevaron hacia el Palacio. Yo quedé inmóvil, sin valor para ir detrás, contemplando la sangre que tenía en las manos. Desde el fondo de las estancias llegaba hasta mí el lloro de las hermanas, y los gritos ya roncos de aquella que clamaba enloquecida:

—¡Fue Satanás . . . ! ¡Fue Satanás . . . !

Sentí miedo. Bajé a las caballerizas y con ayuda de un criado enganché los caballos a la silla de posta. Partí al galope. Al desaparecer bajo el arco de la plaza, volví los ojos llenos de lágrimas para enviarle un adiós al Palacio Gaetani. En la ventana, siempre abierta, me pareció distinguir una sombra trágica y desolada. ¡Pobre sombra envejecida, arrugada, miedosa que vaga todavía por aquellas estancias, y todavía cree verme acechándola en la oscuridad! Me contaron que ahora, al cabo de tantos años, ya repite sin pasión, sin duelo, con la monotonía de una vieja que reza: ¡Fue Satanás!

the stars shone palely, and plummeted to the garden, just when her sister's arms were about to touch her.

"It was Satan! It was Satan!" That anguished cry of María Rosario's still rings in my ears. After so many years I still see her: pale, divine, and tragic as the marble of an antique statue. I still feel the horror of that hour:

"It was Satan! . . . It was Satan! . . ."

The child lay inert on the edge of the front steps. Her face emerged from the veil of her hair as white as a lily, and from her shattered temple oozed the trickle of blood which was soaking that hair. Her sister was shouting like a woman possessed:

"It was Satan! . . . It was Satan! . . ."

I picked up the child, and her sadness-filled eyes opened for a moment. Her bloodied, dying head rolled stiffly onto my shoulder, and her eyes closed again slowly, like twin agonies. Her sister's cries resounded in the silence of the garden:

"It was Satan! . . . It was Satan! . . ."

The golden hair, that head of hair as liquid as light, as fragrant as a garden, was black with blood. I felt it weighing on my shoulder like the fatality of a tragic destiny. With the child in my arms I climbed the stairs. When I was at the top, the anguished chorus of her sisters came out to meet me. I listened to their laments and cries, I felt the mute questioning in those pallid faces, which had terror in their eyes. Their arms stretched out to me desperately, and received their sister's body, and carried it to the palace. I remained motionless, lacking the courage to follow them, gazing at the blood on my hands. From the distant rooms there came to me the weeping of the sisters and the cries, now hoarse, of the one who was calling in madness:

"It was Satan! . . . It was Satan! . . ."

I was afraid. I went down to the stables and, with the help of a servant, I hitched the horses to the post chaise. I departed at a gallop. As I disappeared beneath the arch beside the square, I turned my tear-filled eyes toward the Gaetani palace in a last adieu. In the window, which was still open, I thought I could make out a tragic, desolate shadow. Poor shadow, now old, wrinkled, timorous, which still wanders through those rooms, and still thinks she sees me lying in wait for her in the dark! I've been told that even now, after all those years, she still repeats without passion, without grief, with the monotony of an old woman praying: "It was Satan!"

A CATALOG OF SELECTED
DOVER BOOKS
IN ALL FIELDS OF INTEREST

A CATALOG OF SELECTED DOVER
BOOKS IN ALL FIELDS OF INTEREST

CONCERNING THE SPIRITUAL IN ART, Wassily Kandinsky. Pioneering work by father of abstract art. Thoughts on color theory, nature of art. Analysis of earlier masters. 12 illustrations. 80pp. of text. 5⅜ x 8½.   23411-8

ANIMALS: 1,419 Copyright-Free Illustrations of Mammals, Birds, Fish, Insects, etc., Jim Harter (ed.). Clear wood engravings present, in extremely lifelike poses, over 1,000 species of animals. One of the most extensive pictorial sourcebooks of its kind. Captions. Index. 284pp. 9 x 12.   23766-4

CELTIC ART: The Methods of Construction, George Bain. Simple geometric techniques for making Celtic interlacements, spirals, Kells-type initials, animals, humans, etc. Over 500 illustrations. 160pp. 9 x 12. (Available in U.S. only.)   22923-8

AN ATLAS OF ANATOMY FOR ARTISTS, Fritz Schider. Most thorough reference work on art anatomy in the world. Hundreds of illustrations, including selections from works by Vesalius, Leonardo, Goya, Ingres, Michelangelo, others. 593 illustrations. 192pp. 7⅛ x 10¼.   20241-0

CELTIC HAND STROKE-BY-STROKE (Irish Half-Uncial from "The Book of Kells"): An Arthur Baker Calligraphy Manual, Arthur Baker. Complete guide to creating each letter of the alphabet in distinctive Celtic manner. Covers hand position, strokes, pens, inks, paper, more. Illustrated. 48pp. 8¼ x 11.   24336-2

EASY ORIGAMI, John Montroll. Charming collection of 32 projects (hat, cup, pelican, piano, swan, many more) specially designed for the novice origami hobbyist. Clearly illustrated easy-to-follow instructions insure that even beginning papercrafters will achieve successful results. 48pp. 8¼ x 11.   27298-2

THE COMPLETE BOOK OF BIRDHOUSE CONSTRUCTION FOR WOOD-WORKERS, Scott D. Campbell. Detailed instructions, illustrations, tables. Also data on bird habitat and instinct patterns. Bibliography. 3 tables. 63 illustrations in 15 figures. 48pp. 5¼ x 8½.   24407-5

BLOOMINGDALE'S ILLUSTRATED 1886 CATALOG: Fashions, Dry Goods and Housewares, Bloomingdale Brothers. Famed merchants' extremely rare catalog depicting about 1,700 products: clothing, housewares, firearms, dry goods, jewelry, more. Invaluable for dating, identifying vintage items. Also, copyright-free graphics for artists, designers. Co-published with Henry Ford Museum & Greenfield Village. 160pp. 8¼ x 11.   25780-0

HISTORIC COSTUME IN PICTURES, Braun & Schneider. Over 1,450 costumed figures in clearly detailed engravings–from dawn of civilization to end of 19th century. Captions. Many folk costumes. 256pp. 8⅜ x 11¾.   23150-X

THE STORY OF THE TITANIC AS TOLD BY ITS SURVIVORS, Jack Winocour (ed.). What it was really like. Panic, despair, shocking inefficiency, and a little heroism. More thrilling than any fictional account. 26 illustrations. 320pp. 5⅜ x 8½.
20610-6

FAIRY AND FOLK TALES OF THE IRISH PEASANTRY, William Butler Yeats (ed.). Treasury of 64 tales from the twilight world of Celtic myth and legend: "The Soul Cages," "The Kildare Pooka," "King O'Toole and his Goose," many more. Introduction and Notes by W. B. Yeats. 352pp. 5⅜ x 8½.
26941-8

BUDDHIST MAHAYANA TEXTS, E. B. Cowell and others (eds.). Superb, accurate translations of basic documents in Mahayana Buddhism, highly important in history of religions. The Buddha-karita of Asvaghosha, Larger Sukhavativyuha, more. 448pp. 5⅜ x 8½.
25552-2

ONE TWO THREE . . . INFINITY: Facts and Speculations of Science, George Gamow. Great physicist's fascinating, readable overview of contemporary science: number theory, relativity, fourth dimension, entropy, genes, atomic structure, much more. 128 illustrations. Index. 352pp. 5⅜ x 8½.
25664-2

EXPERIMENTATION AND MEASUREMENT, W. J. Youden. Introductory manual explains laws of measurement in simple terms and offers tips for achieving accuracy and minimizing errors. Mathematics of measurement, use of instruments, experimenting with machines. 1994 edition. Foreword. Preface. Introduction. Epilogue. Selected Readings. Glossary. Index. Tables and figures. 128pp. 5⅜ x 8½.   40451-X

DALÍ ON MODERN ART: The Cuckolds of Antiquated Modern Art, Salvador Dalí. Influential painter skewers modern art and its practitioners. Outrageous evaluations of Picasso, Cézanne, Turner, more. 15 renderings of paintings discussed. 44 calligraphic decorations by Dalí. 96pp. 5⅜ x 8½. (Available in U.S. only.)   29220-7

ANTIQUE PLAYING CARDS: A Pictorial History, Henry René D'Allemagne. Over 900 elaborate, decorative images from rare playing cards (14th–20th centuries): Bacchus, death, dancing dogs, hunting scenes, royal coats of arms, players cheating, much more. 96pp. 9¼ x 12¼.   29265-7

MAKING FURNITURE MASTERPIECES: 30 Projects with Measured Drawings, Franklin H. Gottshall. Step-by-step instructions, illustrations for constructing handsome, useful pieces, among them a Sheraton desk, Chippendale chair, Spanish desk, Queen Anne table and a William and Mary dressing mirror. 224pp. 8⅛ x 11¼.
29338-6

THE FOSSIL BOOK: A Record of Prehistoric Life, Patricia V. Rich et al. Profusely illustrated definitive guide covers everything from single-celled organisms and dinosaurs to birds and mammals and the interplay between climate and man. Over 1,500 illustrations. 760pp. 7½ x 10⅛.   29371-8